No Mountain Too High

Village development in Nepal

16 men carrying 320 kg turbine for 3 days from road head along goat track to micro-hydroelectricity station

Rod Setterlund OAM
In-Country Adviser: Bijaya Rajbhandari

No Mountain Too High: Village Development in Nepal

ISBN: 978-1-922757-83-8 (Paperback)
978-1-922757-84-5 (eBook)

A catalogue record for this book is available from the National Library of Australia

Proofread by: Sarah Kate Hill
Cover Design: Ocean Reeve Publishing
Design and Typeset: Ocean Reeve Publishing
Printed in Nepal by United Multi Printers

Published by Rod Setterlund and Genesis Publishing.
A self-publishing imprint of Ocean Reeve Publishing
www.oceanreevepublishing.com

This book is dedicated to all the 'can do' villagers in the Tawal area and other villages in Nepal.

Contents

Locating Tawal within Nepal

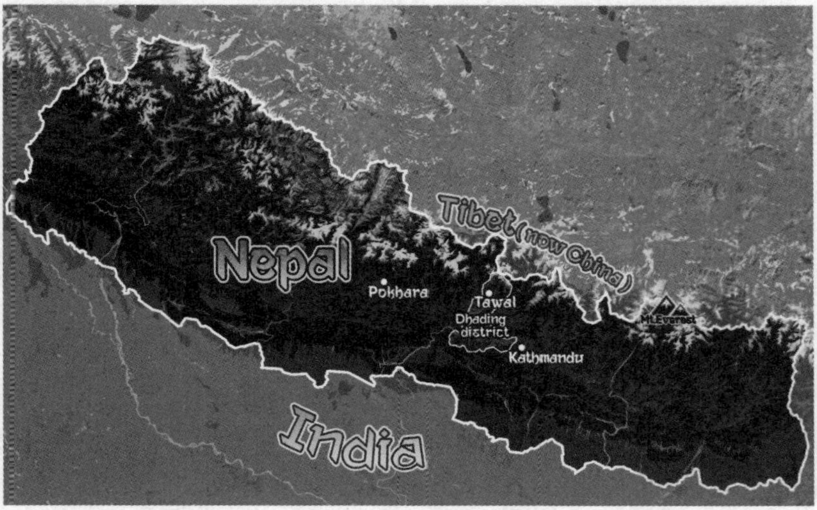

This map has been designed using resources from Flaticon.com

Tawal area

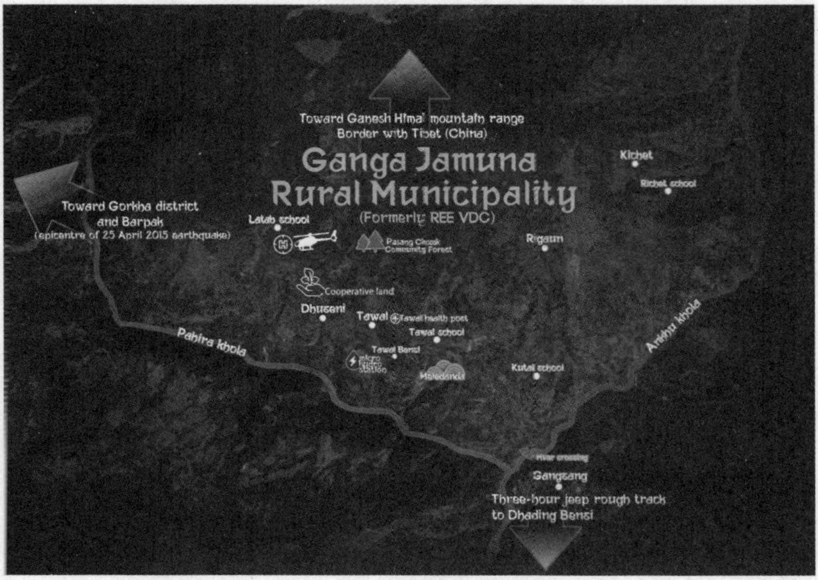

This map has been designed using resources from Flaticon.com

Foreword

On my retirement, I returned to my home country of Nepal. I had spent 36 years with UNICEF, working in various developing countries in Africa, Central Asia, South Asia and East Asia. The work included planning, program and policy development, and implementation in sectors such as water supply, health, education, nutrition and child protection. In early 2018, my wife Binu and I met Rod and Deborah Setterlund through a mutual friend. Rod is President of the Nepal Australia Friendship Association (NAFA) and Deborah its Research and Evaluation Officer.

Rod and Deborah invited us to accompany them on their visit to the Tawal area in April 2018. We had wanted, in retirement, to make some form of contribution to rural development in our home country so jumped at the opportunity. When we first met Rod and Deb in Kathmandu, we were impressed by their humility, their commitment to rural development in Nepal, and their unflinching dedication at an age when many are slowing down. They had been visiting Nepal annually at their own expense for over 10 years.

Binu and I were aware of projects in Nepal that had started well, began to show results, but then lost momentum or ceased operating due to inadequate planning or monitoring. During our visit to Tawal, we witnessed Rod and Deb working in partnership with the local community to identify needs, develop practical solutions, then follow up on their implementation. Following the visit, we were honoured to be asked to take on volunteer positions to provide NAFA with ongoing advice on program development and on the political and social context within which those programs operate.

No Mountain Too High: Village development in Nepal describes how the Tamangs, the predominant group in the Tawal area, migrated to Nepal from Tibet many centuries ago, and how local community leaders yearned to bring education to their communities and to improve the villagers' lives as subsistence farmers. It tells of how a connection between one of these leaders and someone from Brisbane, Australia accelerated the process of development begun by the local community. There were many bureaucratic hurdles to overcome along the way, especially following the devastating 2015 earthquakes.

The impact of the April 2015 earthquake on Tawal area villagers and on the rebuilding of infrastructure and livelihoods is vividly recounted in *No Mountain Too High*. Seemingly insurmountable challenges were met to replace schools in four villages as well as a health post and water and agricultural cooperative infrastructure.

I have been pleased to contribute to this inspiring book, providing comments and advice to Rod on its context. Its story of community development is presented meticulously, sharing development frameworks and experience with other similarly dedicated individuals involved in such work either as paid staff or as volunteers.

The book's unique feature lies in its explanation of how Rod and Deb, through their work with NAFA, successfully connected the needs of the Tawal area with prospective donors back in Australia. They report back regularly to donors, and have even linked local women wanting to increase their income through sewing with consumers in Australia happy to purchase their products! This direct involvement in both need assessment and monitoring of project implementation has encouraged ongoing retention of donors, with the maintenance of donor interest in and enthusiasm for NAFA's work in Nepal.

Successful development requires not only leadership and vision but also an organic relationship between the local community and outside donors. This book illustrates beautifully how such a partnership can address locally identified priorities – education, health, electricity and, more recently, agricultural development – and how vital community participation has been in that development process, ensuring local ownership as opposed to donor-led development.

Development work in Nepal and abroad has been my passion. As an admirer of Rod and Deborah's compassion, drive and love for the Nepalese people over a long period of time, I am honoured to write this foreword. I have read widely on development, but I have never seen a better-written book demonstrating, through a case study of a group of Nepalese villages, how the process of development can be brought to life and maintained, even in the extraordinary times that follow a natural disaster. I am sure you will enjoy the read.

Bijaya Rajbhandari

Introduction

No Mountain Too High is a story with two primary purposes. At its heart, it is a story about an Australian couple's experience of being part of a small, entirely volunteer-run international-aid organisation, the Nepal Australia Friendship Association (NAFA), based in Brisbane, Australia. At the outset, we would like to say that this is not a story about NAFA. That is a great story but a separate one. Rather, this is our personal reflection on how to bring about positive change through community development.

Secondly, and of equal importance, this story is about giving a voice to a group of villagers from an area around Tawal in the hilly region northwest of Kathmandu. These villagers are from the Tamang ethnic group, who migrated south from Tibet at least 300 years ago. In conversations and more recently recorded interviews, they recalled their experiences of development, both the opportunities they created and the struggles they overcame.

This is a story of risk-takers and visionaries who, within a discriminatory social and political context, have always strived for a better life and future for their community. Hunters and gatherers when they first arrived from Tibet, they transitioned to subsistence farming. In 1960, recognising the importance of education to development, villagers volunteered to build a temporary classroom in Tawal; two years later, a grass-roofed, two-room school that went to Grade 3 level was constructed nearby at Meledanda.

"Aphno gau aphno banaune" (Let us build our village ourselves) was a strong conviction for these Tamang villagers. These original schools were built without any government assistance. In 1974, a newer school offering classes up to Grade 5 level was built with government funds and local volunteer labour on the site where the school is now located.

Initially, few children attended school and all were male. Girls stayed at home to help with household chores, collecting wood for cooking, bringing water from the nearby river and caring for younger siblings, while their parents worked in the fields. Future community leaders like Chandra Tamang started their schooling in Meledanda before completing Grade 5 at the newer government school. For some, their parents' 'outside experiences' of living and working in Pokhara, Kathmandu and India seemed to be a catalyst for change, giving them a better appreciation of the potential of education.

After boys completed Grade 5 in Tawal, their parents rented rooms in distant villages so their sons could attend schools that went to Grade 10 level, providing them the opportunity to obtain their School Leaving Certificate. Up to four students shared a room, relying on just enough food from their parents to last for the school week. Chandra says it was a struggle. He and his friends were poor and from a low-status ethnic group, so were treated as outcasts, but they persevered. Most returned to their villages, some becoming important community leaders. Others, like Chandra, found work as trekking porters, taking them well beyond Tawal to far-flung villages. Chandra eventually worked for a trekking agency in Kathmandu and settled there. But Tawal and his Tamang kin remained close to his heart. He remained determined to improve conditions in the area where he grew up.

Back in Tawal, a youth club was formed by local leaders, soon broadening its focus at Chandra's urging to become the Hilly Region Development Club (HRDC). In the late 1990s, an opportunity to access foreign-sourced development funding arose when Chandra, through his trekking work, met Lloyd Magdalinski, a schoolteacher from Brisbane, Australia. Lloyd was then Vice-President of NAFA. In his broken English, Chandra invited Lloyd to visit Tawal, and in 1998, Lloyd became the first Westerner to do so. Lloyd returned to Brisbane with a water infrastructure funding proposal, which was followed by a submission to NAFA and AusAid Kathmandu to co-fund construction of a health post to service several Tawal area villages.

Deb and I had trekked in Nepal in late 1999, and it made a lasting impression. We started to attend NAFA committee meetings, but at the time, Nepal was in the midst of a ten year Maoist insurgency that made it too dangerous to visit many rural areas, including Tawal. We were able to visit Tawal in late 2006, and it soon became clear that a community-development framework could successfully guide a partnership between NAFA and the local community.

Over the next nine years, much progress was made. Then, at midday on Saturday 25 April 2015, the world was changed forever for villagers here and in many other parts of Nepal by a 7.8-magnitude earthquake, its epicentre only 25 km west of Tawal, at Barpak in the Gorkha district. In a matter of minutes, seventy-eight lives in the area were lost and all local infrastructure was destroyed, including approximately 1,225 homes, ten schools, two health posts, a micro-hydro system, and water and agricultural infrastructure. *No Mountain Too High* tells, in the villagers' own words, the experience of that terrible day and its immediate aftermath.

While overseas aid played a part, competent, compassionate Nepalese professionals were critical in helping the community get back on its feet. The story is one of courage, resilience, trust, competency, generosity and persistence. When the Nepalese government failed to honour a promise to undertake geotechnical assessments of all earthquake-affected areas, Dr Dhital, a geotechnical engineer from Kathmandu's Tribhuvan University, responded to a desperate request from the community to visit the area and undertake a rapid assessment for landslide risk. Sabin Shrestha worked tirelessly to prepare site and classroom-design plans for approval by the Nepal Government's Department of Education. Sadit Maharjan left his Kathmandu home to come to the area and oversee the first phase of the daunting program to rebuild four village schools.

Recovery from natural disaster, however, involves more than rebuilding community infrastructure. The local Pasang Chowk Agricultural Cooperative had lost their physical infrastructure in the earthquake. This book tells the yet-to-be completed story of how NAFA and the local community partnered with a compassionate, Brisbane-based philanthropist to re-establish and expand the Agricultural Cooperative. A market-system focussed practice framework was applied, with the intention of providing local villagers a sustainable pathway out of poverty.

This story ends with an analysis of those factors that contribute to positive change in applying community and market-system development approaches. It also identifies the challenges that remain. If you are a curious traveller, a community development practitioner, or have an interest in Nepal, remote village life, or the experiences of communities recovering from disaster, we think you will find *No Mountain Too High* valuable and inspiring.

Chapter 1

I started to dream

Chandra was destined to become a subsistence farmer in Tawal, like his parents. However, after completing Grade 10, a chance meeting changed the course of his life:

> "I was lucky to meet up with a friend from a neighbouring village. He was educated in India, where his father was in the Gurkha Army. He had been working in a tourist hotel in Kathmandu and as a trekking guide. It was so kind of him to rescue me from the village and take me along with him as a trekking porter. It was a great opportunity for me to see a different world. During my porterage work, I was lucky to meet up with nice people from different countries. Since I understood the value of education, I learned to speak some English, knowing how important it was to learn that language."[1]

As Chandra worked his way up from porter to assistant guide, he never forgot his village and the difficulties it faced. He dreamed of finding a way to bring better education and development to the area in which he grew up. While on a trek, he met Lloyd Magdalinski, a high school teacher from Brisbane, Australia:

> "I started to dream. I must change my village and area by educating people there. During my trekking, I was lucky

[1] Occasionally, the English in quotes has been 'tidied up' in this book to ensure the meaning is understood. However, the substantive meaning of quotes has not been changed.

> to meet Mr Lloyd from Brisbane, Australia. He was a schoolteacher there. He used to bring students and their parents to Nepal. I was working as an assistant guide. We became friends. I expressed myself to him, in my poor and broken English and with hands, feet, head and eyes."

On one of the treks, Chandra invited Lloyd to visit Tawal. In addition to being a teacher, Lloyd had started travelling regularly to Nepal to buy handicrafts for resale in Brisbane. He often came during the monsoon season, when few tourists were around. On one such trip, in late August 1998, Lloyd became the first Westerner to visit Tawal. It was a difficult time to trek up to the village.

> "It was not an easy trek up, taking three days, in heavy monsoon rain, in extreme heat and humidity, with landslides, flooded streams, leeches and slippery trails. We slept in a cow shelter between corn-storing baskets, and the sleeping arrangements involved close encounters with local rats. All night, hungry rats ran over us."

Chandra and Lloyd lost the soles of their sodden boots on the trek to Tawal. The problem-solving Chandra remembers:

> "We tied the soles back to the boots with shoelaces and continued trekking."

Lloyd recounted the reaction of villagers on seeing him, the first Westerner to visit the area.

> "The first sight of a tall, white person drew a curious audience. Most of the people from the village had never seen a white man. They wondered why I was there. Some of the children were afraid I might be a child-eating monster!"

Chandra explains that the children had a particular reason to be curious.

> "Lloyd had a roll of pink toilet paper with him, and it was the first time most people in the village had seen toilet paper. The children were fascinated and wanted to follow him behind the bushes to see how it was used!"

During his visit to Tawal, Lloyd experienced warmth and friendliness, but also describes a village in dire need:

> "I remember seeing villagers who were poor and dirty. The children were a particularly sad sight – few clothes and poor health conditions. Many children, especially girls, were not attending the dark, damp school that existed in the village, because they had to fetch water for their family from the local river every morning."

Although Chandra had difficulty with the finer points of English, he could see the impression the village was having on Lloyd:

> "At the time, my English was not good enough to explain all the problems there. He understood the needs of the village and reported this to kind and supportive NAFA members back in Australia."

Lloyd had a natural inclination to approach village problems through consultation and joint decision-making, a forerunner of the community development approach we would adopt years later. One of the main reasons for the poor school attendance was the lack of accessible water, requiring school-age children to collect water for their families daily.

Together, local leaders indicated that:

> "water was the priority – we needed to bring water from the river to the village, so it was there for families".

Lloyd returned to Brisbane with a water infrastructure proposal, which he presented at NAFA's October 1998 management committee meeting. Six reserve tanks and nine water taps would bring water from the nearby Kalsyong Khola to 320 households in Tawal and the adjoining villages of Dhuseni and Sherchet. NAFA committee members agreed that this was a suitable project for their support, and the Tawal water infrastructure project was approved.

Less than a year later, Chandra was successful in attracting an Austrian couple, Guenther Stummvoll and Christa Sprenger, to Tawal. Like Lloyd, they encountered a village without basic facilities, inhabited by people who led hard lives but still found pleasure in daily life:

> "Walking up the last hill we could see Tawal for the first time. The village, with the stone houses and slate roofs, was so beautiful and peaceful, embedded in the fields around the area. We loved this place from the first moment.
>
> Arriving at the village we were overwhelmed by the welcome ceremony. We felt we were the first foreigners local people had ever seen. No teahouse or lodge existed in the village. Life was going on like in the Middle Ages. Extremely hard. But all the people seemed to enjoy life much more than we in the so-called developed countries are able to do."

However, Guenther and Christa were dismayed by the condition of the school:

> "Seeing the school building, we could not believe 150 children were having lessons in such a building. The classrooms were dark and rarely bigger than 10 square metres for 30 children. Only two teachers for 150 children – from this moment, we knew a lot of help would be necessary to make the dream for a better education come true. It would take time – perhaps 20 years."

After talking with Chandra, Guenther and Christa committed to raise funds to build classrooms so that the school could extend to Grades 6 and 7. They also offered to sponsor a teacher in Tawal and two in the nearby villages of Kutal and Dhuseni. The teacher in Tawal, Lal Maya Tamang, became the first female teacher employed in the Ree Village Development Committee (VDC) area. The link to foreigners with the capacity and compassion to raise funds for the area had been made.

In Tawal, local leaders, including Bhim Tamang, Dipak Tamang, Akal Tamang and Bhakta Tamang, had established the People Awareness Youth Club. This was an initiative to advocate for the rights of young people during a period when there was democracy in Nepal. It started by doing practical work such as constructing a playground and putting up a volleyball net. Local leaders tried to register the club at the district level but were rejected. An established registration process for such self-help groups did not exist at the time.

Leaders of the youth club met with Chandra, who even then had a deep sense of community and equity. In those early days, he envisioned working collectively with other villages in the area, bringing people together to address community-wide issues. He advised the youth club leaders to broaden their focus from young people to the whole Tawal community and beyond, including nearby villages. As a result, the volunteer-run Hilly Region Development Club (HRDC) was established, with Chandra elected its first president. The HRDC proved to be a driving force for change, and over twenty years later continues to play a central role in the development of the Tawal area.

Lloyd again visited Tawal in February 2000 to inspect the water infrastructure project and to open two new classrooms funded by Guenther and Christa. Lloyd also met with the recently formed HRDC committee. With Lloyd and Chandra's help, the HRDC developed a local Integrated Plan of Projects. The plan listed the priority areas (water infrastructure, transport, education and health) at that time, identified actual or proposed funding sources, and flagged the role that donors could potentially play in developing the area.

The Integrated Plan was developed by village leaders acutely aware of community values and priorities: the interconnectedness of education, health and other community infrastructure; a willingness to contribute their own labour to projects; and a desire to partner with outsiders to change their communities for the better. They had an innate sense of the principles and processes that form the building blocks of community development. The Integrated Plan was the forerunner of the community development approach driven by us, with funding from NAFA.

The plan involved the development of basic services taken for granted by residents of first-world countries. Such services in countries like Australia are largely funded by the government, but this is not the case in Nepal and many other developing countries. Villagers knew that to develop, they had to do so without government assistance, and where possible in partnership with outside donors. In the Integrated Plan, villagers recognised NAFA's limited funds and therefore looked

Key components of the 2000 HRDC Integrated Plan of Projects		
Water infrastructure and transport	**Education**	**Health**
Water infrastructure Water-reserve tanks, pipes and taps in the villages of: • Tawal • Dhuseni • Sherchet – funded by NAFA	Additional/ replacement classrooms in old school at Tawal – funded by Guenther Stummvoll and Christa Sprenger (Austria) – funded by NAFA	Health post servicing six villages – successful submission to AusAid, Kathmandu for co-funding with NAFA
Transport Suspension bridge for safe crossing of Ankhu Khola (subsequently funded and installed by Kadoorie Charitable Foundation, welfare arm of Gurkha soldiers)	School notebooks and pens for children attending school – funding by customers of Namaste (Lloyd's shop in Brisbane that sold Nepalese products)	Training of health-care worker – sponsored by a doctor in Brisbane
	Adult literacy – funding by customers of Namaste	Health post salaries – funded by NAFA, with a proposal at the time by Lloyd and Chandra that the salaries be funded from two social enterprises: silk production and a solar telephone
	School to eventually be extended to Grade 10 – funding sources unknown at the time	Medicine for health post – self-funded through charges to villagers for medicine provided to them at the health post

to a variety of possible funding sources. Chandra would be the link to those resources through his own newly established trekking agency in Kathmandu, Nepal Experienced Adventure Treks (NEAT). Lloyd presented the Integrated Plan to the NAFA committee at its February 2000 meeting. The committee decided to focus on the health priority and considered a proposal to construct a health post at Tawal, the largest village in the VDC.

By April 2000, NAFA was informed that villagers had taken the initiative, within their limited resources. Lloyd reported that:

> "The Tawal community had purchased the land and were hard at work (using volunteer labour) levelling the site for the health post."

A doctor in Brisbane whose son Lloyd taught had sponsored a young local woman, Nima Tamang, to undertake an eighteen-month (plus practicum) Community Medicine Assistant course. Nima was to staff the health post when construction was completed. Another young man, Beg Tamang, from the nearby village of Kutal, began family-funded study in the same course not long after, the plan being that he would assist Nima as a second health worker.

At NAFA's April 2000 meeting, a partnership with AusAid in their Kathmandu office to jointly fund construction of the health post was approved. Minutes from the meeting stated that the committee also agreed to pay "salaries for the health-care worker and an assistant until 2003, when hopefully the health post will be self-sustainable".

Chandra was advised of NAFA's in-principle offer to co-fund construction of the health post and the requirements of "eventual self-sustainability". Chandra and the villagers were worried about signing up to a commitment they could not meet.

Chandra faxed Lloyd, telling him that:

> "A meeting of the village committee confirmed their willingness for the health post to be self-sustained. However, as Tawal does not generate much of an income, they are unsure how this could be achieved and therefore did not want to commit to the building until they could see a way of earning the money needed to pay for the health post's running costs."

The fax was discussed by NAFA committee members, who came up with two ideas for income generation to fund the health project. Minutes of the meeting recorded:

> "Lloyd felt that the installation of the solar telephone would generate income, along with expected profit from [the] new silk-farming project, or an approach would be made to the Nepal Government for funds. It was decided that money raised at NAFA's next 'Hike to Help' fundraising event would be utilised in the setting up of the solar phone."

The then-President of NAFA advised Lloyd to tell Chandra that NAFA would meet the shortfall in health post wages if the community demonstrated a genuine inability to meet those costs. The issue of self-sustainability is a challenging one for aid agencies supporting projects in developing countries. It would prove to be particularly so for NAFA and other funding partners of two multi-year programs in the Tawal area, one subsidising health-worker salaries and the other subsidising teacher salaries (more on these challenges later in the book). NAFA was justifiably proud of its support for this health initiative. However, within its limited resources, it could not fund other components of the Integrated Plan, with the result that the plan fell off the NAFA agenda.

In February 2001, neither Lloyd nor Chandra was able to visit Tawal, as the Maoists controlled the area. Lloyd's report to the NAFA committee included a sad footnote:

> "Just been notified that after completing her studies, Nima was fatally injured in a bus accident. She was returning to Tawal to take up duties at the health post when the accident occurred."

Chapter 2

You start walking from here, Didi

Beg Tamang completed his rural health studies in 2001, but Maoist control of the area caused delays in completing construction of the health post until the following year. Lloyd reported that the Nepalese Army had briefly cleared the area and villagers were returning to Tawal from the army-controlled district capital of Dhading Bensi. While NAFA projects were continuing in the area, the Maoist insurgency had set back the development agenda just when health and education standards were starting to improve. It would be another five years before it was safe for foreigners to visit the Tawal area again. It was also unsafe for Chandra to visit the village he grew up in. As manager of his small trekking agency, he was at risk of being kidnapped for ransom by the Maoists.

Fear gripped the rural villages under Maoist control. Students, teachers and members of the community were forced to attend Maoist training camps for ideological indoctrination. There was also ongoing pressure to join the Maoist Army and even abductions of students for recruitment. Maoists demanded medicine from health post workers. Teachers and health post workers were forced to pay 5% of their salaries to the Maoists. In true entrepreneurial spirit, they negotiated the extortion 'tax' down from the countrywide standard of 10%!

Local leaders described the difficulty of life during the Maoist insurgency.

> "The Maoist time was a nightmare. Maoists came from other areas and lived in the community, staying at people's houses, no choice for the locals. Coming from

> outside the area, they would be able to coerce locals to join without having family obligations or feelings of empathy. 'Our home was their home.' We had to put up with this for 10 years.
>
> The Maoists were armed and used telescopes to look for the Nepalese Army. When they saw they were coming, they would disappear into the forest above Tawal.
>
> The Maoists interrogated local leaders of the newly established Youth Club, but let them go after the leaders showed them they had no money and were interested only in improving the rights and resources available to young people.
>
> People were beaten and threatened. The Maoists suspected locals were collaborating with the Nepalese Army by spying on them. Soldiers from the Nepalese Army beat people for the same reason.
>
> All the students from Rigaun, a village above Tawal, were taken by the Maoists for two days' training in Maoist ideology and how to make bombs, etc. Children felt unsafe and some young men even went to foreign countries."

Chandra's nephew Yuddha tells how the Maoists affected him, his family and other villagers in the area:

> "I was attending Grade 6 in Gumdi [four to five hours' walk from Tawal], where a number of students would rent a room for the school week, when the Maoists first came to the school there. They talked to students, telling them about Maoist ideology. They tried to convince us to join them. I changed schools in Grade 8, going up to

a school at Rigaun. The Maoists came to our home and demanded food. They took teachers and students, boys and girls, away for propaganda camps. Parents were really scared. My parents moved to Dhading Bensi because of the Maoist problem when I was in Grade 9. My father was involved in politics at the time. He had been President of the VDC a few years before, and we were worried because the Maoists had killed other politicians.

While in Grade 10, I was asked by the Nepalese Army to spy on the student Maoists. Students came from many villages to Dhading Bensi to get extra tuition in the lead-up to the SLC exams. The army would come and search our rooms. We had to show proof we were students. One of the officers gave me his phone number and said I had to call him if I suspected any students were Maoists.

I once met a Maoist politician, Ganesh Tamang from Darkha VDC. His vision was clear and good. In his speeches he talked about the importance of Tamang culture and teaching school in Tamang language. He used to say, 'How can we be good in Nepali or English language if we are not good in Tamang language?' But the Maoists killed him because he was becoming too popular."

A teacher expressed his feelings on the impact that one encounter with Maoists had on his wife when she was a student at Tawal.

"My wife was in Grade 6 and was kidnapped by the Maoists for three days. Her family stopped her from continuing at school for fear of her being kidnapped again. She now regrets that – damage is so long-lasting. I am also bitter about this, as it prevented my wife from going higher in her education."

It was a particularly hard time for Beg, coordinator at the health post, who was under constant pressure from both the Maoists and the Nepalese Army. He treated whoever needed his help, be they local villagers, Maoists or soldiers from the Nepalese Army. He was at constant risk of being beaten, or worse, for treating members of the 'other side'. At one point, it became so dangerous that Chandra invited him to Kathmandu for his own safety. But Beg stayed, knowing local villagers needed him. He even closed the health post after one group of Maoists said it had to be registered with them. But another Maoist group found out the health post was closed and demanded that Beg reopen it! In the end, the health post at Tawal survived, as it was built by outside donors and operated independently of the government.

Local leaders told us that during the Maoist insurgency, a rural health worker, Abinandan Chaudhari, from the Terai region in southern Nepal, came to the area to work on a government quota. While working at the health post in Salleri, he was captured by the Maoists. After he refused (or was unable) to meet their demands, he was killed, and his body was thrown off the cliff near the current Tawal school. The ten-year Maoist insurgency claimed the lives of over 17,000 people, as well as displacing hundreds of thousands from rural areas. Most moved to Kathmandu, which was considered safer.

Since my teen years in Canada, I had dreamt of trekking in Nepal, and in November 1999, amid the civil war, I finally fulfilled this dream. Lloyd connected Deb and me with Chandra and his trekking agency. He organised the 'Ghorepani trek' for us, a common introductory trek in the Annapurna range north of Pokhara. Chandra met us on arrival at the airport in Kathmandu. As we drove into Kathmandu, we looked over at each other, more than a little overwhelmed by what we were seeing from the car windows. There was so much activity of daily life in the streets, including men shaving and women washing.

We thought we had seen poverty in countries such as Mexico, but this was different.

After settling into our hotel, we walked over to Chandra's office. He rose to greet us, his wide smile and alert brown eyes soothing any anxieties we were feeling about our impending eight-day trek. Fielding phone calls with one hand, deftly extracting passport photos and trekking permits from a file with the other, he was a man on a mission. We noted the ribbon-tied folder and the notes he had added to the typed itinerary of our trek. The system was basic, but the man was not. Potential logistical problems were quickly addressed and resolved, and the details of our trek carefully explained. Chandra means 'moon' in Nepali. Did his parents know their bright-eyed son would one day shine a welcome light on his birthplace, Tawal village?

The trek made a lasting impression on us. The sheer beauty of the country, the compact and picturesque remote villages, and the warmth, friendliness and openness of the villagers touched our hearts. But we were also struck by the poverty. We had not anticipated the effect this would have on us. Lloyd had told us he was a member of a charity in Brisbane which was raising funds for small projects in Nepal. We decided to find out more and attended our first NAFA meeting in April 2000.

We returned to Nepal in March 2001 for a trek to Everest Base Camp. After the trek, Deb presented a paper at a 'Health and Wellbeing Conference' in Kathmandu. The conference was opened by Her Royal Highness Princess Sruti Rajya Laxmi Devi Rana, and the Princess and Deb exchanged 'namastes'. Two months later, we were driving home to Brisbane from a weekend of hiking at Girraween National Park, in the Granite Belt south of Brisbane. Through the crackling car radio, we heard the words "massacre in Nepal" and pulled over. It was 1 June 2001. Princess Sruti had been killed in the royal palace, together with her father, King Birendra, her mother, Queen Aishwarya, and nine others. Ironically, after shooting himself, the alleged perpetrator of the massacre, Crown Prince Dipendra, though in a coma, was declared king before he died three days later. Birendra's brother, Gyanendra, then became king.

I took on the position of NAFA Treasurer in 2003. We returned to Nepal that year, and the next, to do the Annapurna 'round' and Annapurna base-camp treks. King Gyanendra had a more confrontational approach to the Maoist insurgency than had King Birendra. By 2004, conditions in the country were deteriorating. Most businesses in Kathmandu and family-run lodges on the trekking routes were being extorted by the Maoists. On 1 February 2005, in response to the inability of the democratic government to restore order, King Gyanendra seized full control of the government with the explicit aim of ending the insurgency.

In November 2005, we travelled again to Nepal, this time to trek to the stunning, high-altitude lake at Gokyo Ri, in the Everest area. However, conditions in Nepal continued to deteriorate. In April 2006, King Gyanendra was forced to return power to parliament after massive street demonstrations. His status was reduced to that of a ceremonial monarch. We arrived in Nepal in September 2006 to trek to Lo Mantang in Mustang, northwest of Jomsom in the Annapurnas.

In our early visits to Nepal, we were on a steep learning curve, not only about the people, the culture and the day-to-day sights, but also about our own reactions to what we were experiencing. Walking around the bustling streets of Kathmandu is both fascinating and troubling. The smell of piles of rotting garbage due to a refuse collectors' strike, sleeping street children huddled in a dirty blanket in front of a yet-to-open upmarket store, and smooth-talking men offering drugs for sale tastefully displayed in the different pockets of their safari jackets are all part of daily Kathmandu life. In the Maoist days, we quickened our pace as we passed groups of heavy-booted, grim-faced soldiers striding the streets of Kathmandu and Pokhara.

While we were in Nepal, there was a political breakthrough when a seven-party alliance, including the Maoists, released a twelve-point agreement that brought a pause in hostilities. Political parties agreed to hold elections for a constituent assembly and draft a new federal constitution. Agreement on that constitution would take another ten years! An interim parliament had been formed that brought the Maoists into the political mainstream. The decade-long insurgency came to an end with the signing of the Comprehensive National Peace Treaty by Prime Minister Girija Prasad Koirala and Maoist chairman Puspa Kamal Dahal aka Prachanda on 21 November 2006.

We had completed our trek but were still in Nepal for this historic occasion. We decided to extend our visas, and Chandra organised our first visit to Tawal. We were interested in other NAFA-supported projects, such as the remote cataract eye-surgery clinics and a children's home in Kathmandu. But this was also an opportunity to see for ourselves what was happening in Tawal, a village Lloyd had been so passionate about in meetings when we first became involved in NAFA.

We left Kathmandu before daylight and travelled by car to the district capital, Dhading Bensi. Accompanying us was our guide, Kami Lama, who was from Tawal, and another NAFA executive officer. We stopped for morning tea at the home of Chandra's sister, Ganga, and her husband, Akal. When we were ready to go, Deb asked Ganga, "Where do we start trekking?", assuming that the road went at least partially in the direction we were heading. "You start walking from here, Didi," Ganga answered! Deb was suitably chastened.

We trekked up, up, up for six hours, until dusk, camping at a spot where we could see in the distance the beautiful Ganesh Himal mountain range bordering Tibet. The second day was tough – eleven hours of trekking, including five hours over stones in the blazing sun, along the Ankhu Khola. At dusk, we crossed a suspension bridge built by the Gurkhas. Tired and hot, we thought we were going to camp along the riverbed. However, unbeknown to us, an ancient Bon Buddhist festival, 'Ekadashi Jatra', was starting that night in Tawal. Kami and the porters were keen to get there, and gently willed us to keep going. We dragged ourselves up an 800-metre climb to Tawal from the river, the last hour from Kutal in total darkness, with only our headlamps illuminating the stone pathway. We arrived dehydrated and totally spent.

A traditional horn and drum band met us at the entrance to Tawal and led us to Chandra's parents' house in the village. We were greeted by Chandra's father and mother, who thereafter would be known to us as 'hazurbaa' (grandfather) and 'hajuraama' (grandmother). We sat down on the hard-packed earthen floor and were welcomed with a cup of warm buffalo milk. It was not easy to drink warm milk after the hot, exhausting trek up from the river, but I did so respectfully. Deb quietly set her cup down, fearing that being sick would offend our proud and distinguished hosts. We were then taken up to the monastery above the village to bed down for the night.

Due to the Maoist insurgency, it was the first time in six years that Westerners had visited Tawal. We awoke to eyes peering through the monastery windows, curious children and adults watching us unpack our backpacks. They were very shy in those early days and spoke no English. When Deb started up her electric toothbrush, they gathered around, giggling and pointing.

Children at the school greeted us with 'khatas', ceremonial scarves traditionally presented to guests in this part of Nepal. A dance program featured a traditional Tamang welcome song and a gender awareness-raising dance that encouraged parents to send their daughters to school. After the program, we distributed to very appreciative children from Nursery to Grade 4 warm, brightly coloured jumpers and beanies knitted by women in Brisbane.

We were moved by the children's enthusiasm and openness. But we shared Guenther and Christa's alarm about the state of the classrooms: dark and damp, with water dripping down the walls onto clay floors. Students sat crowded on wooden benches, keen to learn but in a learning environment that was untenable. We left the school determined to advocate that NAFA join Guenther and Christa in raising funds to replace the classrooms.

Visiting the health post that had been built five years before with funding from NAFA and AusAid, Kathmandu, we met with the three health workers: Beg, Lila Maya and Sunita. We watched in awe as Beg stitched a large gash over the eye of a man who had fallen and struck his head on a rock. On another visit, an eight-year-old girl arrived at the health post with a big gash on her chin. Beg stitched her up, at that time without anaesthetic! Only a tear came down the cheek of this brave little girl, and she and her dad went away happy. We were to witness the value of Beg's medical skills on many occasions.

This trip to Tawal made a strong impression on us. We were to put energy into other NAFA projects based in the Kathmandu valley and in Pokhara. But this experience initiated our interest and determination over the next fifteen years to make a difference to the lives of villagers in the Tawal area.

Chapter 3

More than good intentions

During our first visit to the Tawal area, in 2006, and two further visits, in early and late 2008, we were eager to get to know this community and find out how they were faring after years of Maoist control. We sat in a circle in the schoolyard. A meeting with HRDC members during our November 2008 visit shaped our idea of the most effective approach to take in future. Looking somewhat 'Leprechaunish' in the hand-knitted lime-green beanies gifted to us by the villagers, we explored HRDC representatives' hopes for the future.

In those early meetings, we were unaware of the Integrated Plan the HRDC had developed eight years earlier. We also gave no thought to the possibility that there was already a history of self-help in the area. Although not consciously, we undoubtedly were working from the 'Western-centric' worldview that it takes a Westerner to really get things going and that development largely comes through outside aid. We knew Tawal villagers were 'can do' people, but only later did we discover their history of managing their own lives and initiating change in their community. These efforts had endured despite a subsistence farming existence, lack of resources, government indifference and social discrimination towards the Tamang and other ethnic groups.

Looking back, we are conscious of how little we knew at that time about Tamang people as one of Nepal's 160 ethnic groups and their unique history. We had gained an overview of Nepal's complex and rich national history from our *Lonely Planet* book on Nepal. But our introduction to Tamangs would come from Chandra, a born storyteller. Sitting around the kitchen table when we had been invited to dinner, Chandra told us tales of his childhood. As a small boy, living high above Tawal in a rough shelter near the jungle with his grandparents, he learnt to forage for wild food and hunt for birds to fill the family dinner pot. Clothing was all hand made by his grandmother from *allo,* the stems of the Giant Himalayan stinging nettle bush. Life involved relentless hard work but was always full of adventure for an enthusiastic boy like Chandra, always eager to learn new skills.

With our keen interest in politics, we kept abreast of the twists and turns of Nepal's governance and its impact on ethnic groups like Tamangs. However, it was not until 2013 and the years afterwards that we developed a deep understanding of Tamang history in the Tawal area. At that time, village leaders expressed concern that their local history was being lost. Deb offered to collect and record the elders' stories. This oral history, which took over six years to collect, became the foundation for a book written by Deb: *Where the Tiger Lives: a Tamang oral history*. A few quotes from villagers who participated in Deborah's oral history research have been used in this book.

We were honoured to witness a traditional dance by elders in the dimly lit centre square of Tawal one night during our visit. During the dance, elders still sing a song, *Maane Dori*, that tells (chants) the story of their forefathers' journey from Utsang, Tibet, passing five Tibetan gompas before crossing the Kyirong Pass on the border of Tibet and Nepal, and then passing another 30 gompas before eventually settling in the Tawal area. Their ancestors first lived in caves, then built rough huts, transitioning from hunter-gatherers to subsistence farmers.

The elders' stories show that a hunter-gatherer lifestyle was a complex endeavour, requiring integration of their spiritual beliefs, Indigenous knowledge and practices, and reciprocal social relationships. Although humiliated by higher-caste groups in the outside world and fearful of Hindu officials who visited their villages, discrimination was unknown among Tamangs. In every facet of their lives, Buddhist beliefs and an egalitarian social system helped them live harmoniously, and the conversion of some to Christianity, while challenging, ultimately did not upset this balance.

Thinking back on our meetings in 2008 sitting with the HRDC members, Tamang history in the Tawal area villages was starkly evident in the dilapidated state of the old classrooms, overcrowding, the hand-to-mouth existence of subsistence farming, and reliance on poorly paid basket making as the main source of income. There was no electricity, no extensive field irrigation or modern farming practices that could produce higher-value crops. There was little or no help from government agencies for development purposes; yet villagers were hopeful that they could improve their lives.

As we listened to the villagers and learned more about the issues, it was clear the HRDC would require a NAFA commitment for multi-year funding in health and education. Implicitly, they were 'inviting' NAFA to partner with them to bring about transformative change to their villages. The way the HRDC operated, supported by Chandra in Kathmandu, impressed us. It worked inclusively, thinking about villages as clusters, thus including representatives from five villages in the area. The HRDC was establishing an impressive track record of getting things done. The health post, the work of the health workers and the new classrooms recently built within budget were testament to that.

On the ground, the HRDC was intuitively doing 'community development' but lacked the resources to accelerate the process. It became clear to us that the cluster of villages around Tawal would be an ideal area for conscious use of a community development approach. Guided by that aid framework, we could identify needs; assess, negotiate and fund projects that would address those needs; then evaluate the outcomes of our projects in different sectors, such as education, health, the environment and economic development. Over time, we believed this area could become NAFA's 'showcase' for its development-aid efforts in Nepal.

In 2004, NAFA had obtained AusAid and Australian Tax Office approval of Deductible Gift Recipient (tax-deductible) status, selecting 'development' as the criterion for the focus of NAFA's aid projects in Nepal. I prepared the section of the submission for tax deductibility that set out key principles in NAFA's development framework. A community development approach was consistent with contemporary United Nations (UN) and Australian Government AusAid approaches to international aid. However, it was a new approach for NAFA. At the time, we did not anticipate the level of push-back that would arise from some members about providing much of NAFA's aid focus in the one area. We would soon need to address that concern. How we did that and whether we could have done better will be discussed later.

At the time, however, we did not have a long-term plan. We simply wanted to make a positive difference and knew that guiding our efforts required a sound theoretical framework. Effective overseas aid requires more than good intentions. It should incorporate a framework for best practice that leads to better outcomes for those benefiting from the aid, particularly those most disadvantaged.

For us, visits to the Tawal area began a slow process of learning more about the community, building relationships with local leaders, and identifying their priorities and proposed solutions for improving their community. During each visit, we would meet with key groups, initially HRDC members, teachers, and health workers – later, women and members of the local Dalit community. We also joined in festivals and other community activities that took place during our visits. At the time, we did not envisage that these visits would build momentum beyond an initial focus on health and education, leading to accelerated multi-sectoral development, including economic development.

Deb and I had both studied and applied community development principles in our work lives. AusAID advocated community development practice. NAFA's focus on health and education projects at that time was also consistent with the 2000 UN Millennium Development goals promoting universal primary education (Goal 2), gender equality and women's empowerment (Goal 3), reducing child mortality (Goal 4) and improving maternal health (Goal 5). Future NAFA projects in the area would promote environmental sustainability (Goal 7).

So, what do we mean by 'community development'? In UN and other authoritative declarations, community development is seen as a human right. While there is no one agreed-upon definition, the declarations have wordings that are consistent with AusAID's definition that provided a useful guide at the time of NAFA's submission for tax-deductibility status:

> "A comprehensive economic, social, cultural and political process which aims at the constant improvement of the wellbeing of the entire population and of all individuals on the basis of their active, free and meaningful participation in development and in the fair distribution of the benefits that result from this process."

Proponents stress that the process or manner in which community development is practised is as important as the quantifiable outcomes or results of the efforts applied. Community development also encompasses such human-rights principles as: participation, inclusiveness, relationships, responsibility and accountability. Other principles said to be crucial to effective and ethical community development practice include:

- Primacy of community interests: community interests should primarily drive projects.
- Need for negotiation: priorities and preferred solutions need to be negotiated between a community and the funding organisation, based on a feasibility assessment of needs, options that address those needs, and the resource capacity of the funding organisation.
- Cultural competence: an ability to interact effectively with people of different cultures and socioeconomic backgrounds is critical.
- Strengths and capacity-building: individual and community knowledge and abilities to identify, assess and act on issues of concern to them should be enhanced.
- Leadership: qualities and expertise of local leaders should be identified and strengthened, including vision for the future; integrity and honesty; community trust in applying good governance principles; and collaborating with and balancing the expectations of the community.
- Sustainability: longer-term benefits should be attained through the process.

Putting these principles into practice requires a framework. Our community development framework has been adapted from community development literature, including a textbook which Deb co-wrote.[2] The various phases of the framework are depicted in

[2] O'Connor, I., Wilson, J., Setterlund, D. and Hughes, M. (2008) Social Work and Human Service Practice, 5th ed. Pearson Education, Frenchs Forest, NSW

the diagram below, with an explanation of the terms following the diagram.

Phases in the community development process

Understanding context

Locate a community within its complex social, cultural, political and economic environment, seeking deeper explanations and testing assumptions.

Developing relationships

Spend time building trust, practising cultural competence and strengthening relationships.

Strengthening local capacity

Value and utilise local knowledge and expertise, identifying local change-makers, and strengthening the local capacity of those change-makers, other leaders and those who benefit from the process.

Identifying needs and priorities

Share information, identify and negotiate needs and priorities through listening (not telling), especially for the most disadvantaged.

Assessing and agreeing on solutions

Identify and assess possible solutions that address identified needs within available resources.

Working across sectors

Where practical, integrate identified solutions in sectors such as health, education, the environment and economic development.

Encouraging participation and ownership

Incorporate local contributions to project planning, decision-making, implementation and helping meet the cost of projects (including in-kind donations such as volunteer labour).

Organising and implementing

Plan and implement tasks and timelines.

Monitoring and evaluating

Develop baseline data, measuring and monitoring change over time where possible, evaluate how solutions have been implemented, being consistent but flexible, and undertake continuous reflection on what needs improvement.

Our focus early on was to develop relationships with HRDC members, teachers and health workers, who collectively would represent community interests in the emerging partnership with NAFA. We had come to Tawal knowing that HRDC members already had a positive, albeit introductory relationship with Lloyd

Magdalinski. They also had great trust in Chandra, who was their link with foreign donors. We wanted to ensure that villagers had ample opportunity to express their viewpoints and to be in control of identifying their priorities and proposed solutions. This was not as straightforward as it first appeared.

Communication has always been and will continue to be a challenge. In the late 1990s, Lloyd and Chandra communicated by post. When urgent communication was required, it was done by fax (costly from Nepal). Communication between Chandra in Kathmandu and village leaders in Tawal was equally challenging.

Mobile phone reception in the village came in 2007, a year after our first visit to the area. In the early days, coverage was intermittent and, for subsistence farmers, the cost was quite high, so take-up was slow. However, in recent years, Nepal Telecom Corporation constructed a mobile phone tower across the valley from Tawal, improving reception. With the import from China of cheaper mobile phones, every household in the area now has a mobile phone. They have become important for connecting family members working in the fields with those in the village and for connecting with family outside the village. Nevertheless, mobile phone recharge cards remain an expensive component of a villager's monthly budget.

Connection to the internet followed the introduction of mobile phones but requires a special, expensive device; 4G is not yet available. The government has contracted one service provider, Subisu, to provide an internet service to the Ward Office and the school. But as neither the Cooperative nor the HRDC has been allowed to connect to Subisu, internet speeds remain antiquated. This makes email communication difficult, especially trying to download attachments.

So from 2008 to 2015, we were attempting to apply a community development approach with only brief (three- to four-day) visits to the area, when we would work directly with people in an intense way, supplemented by much indirect work via email with Chandra. It was challenging and never ideal. New proposals were usually identified during our visits to the village. However, Chandra was a key change-maker in his own right, often coming up with new ideas in Kathmandu and sharing them by phone with village leaders. If village leaders agreed that the idea was a priority, Chandra would test the idea with us by email. For example, the idea of a multipurpose room at the school, comprising a computer lab, library and community meeting space, came from Chandra and was adopted enthusiastically by teachers and HRDC members. The need to communicate from afar with local leaders when monitoring project implementation has been equally challenging. In the early years, issues inevitably arose and had to be relayed to us via Chandra in Kathmandu. Our follow-up queries then had to be relayed back to the village via Chandra.

During our visits to the area, meetings often need to be scheduled to fit in with the villagers' harvesting season. Some HRDC members have to come from Latab, an hour's walk away, to attend meetings, which inevitably start late. Sometimes, meeting attendance would be large, while at other times, mainly the leaders would show up. Our photos and records over the years show high attendance at HRDC and public meetings when the agenda focussed on initiatives the community considered particularly important. This included meetings attended by more than 300 villagers to discuss the feasibility of the proposed micro-hydroelectricity system (Chapter 6) and the possible introduction of more efficient cooking stoves (Chapter 8).

We found that although there were female representatives on the HRDC, women rarely came to meetings. This made strengthening relationships with local women leaders difficult. When we asked where the women were, they always seemed to be 'out of the village' or 'busy with harvesting' or involved in 'family business'. By continuing to ask that the women attend, we were communicating the importance of female participation in village development. Women started to attend meetings and, gradually, began to speak up. But Deb eventually decided that the best way to give women a stronger voice was to meet with them separately (see Chapter 16).

While the national language is Nepali, many of the older people speak only their mother tongue – Tamang. Some of our guides over the years were from the area and would translate chunks of our sentences into Tamang. Often, after much had been exchanged in Tamang, what appeared to be a consensus view arising from that discussion would be translated back into English. Much of the detail was undoubtedly lost in translation. How much more informative it would have been to understand what was being said in those deeper conversations. We tried but, sadly, attaining fluency in either Nepali or the local dialect of the Tamang language was beyond us. We did rely a lot on body language to gauge the feelings in the room and were mindful to monitor our own.

We also were aware that we put a lot of trust in the translator to accurately represent what we had said and the responses from those attending the meeting. This meant that our relationship with a guide/translator was particularly important. Yuddha Tamang, Chandra's nephew, has been a particularly good translator. He knew the local language and understood well what we were trying to achieve in the area.

> "Villagers prefer Tamang language even though they speak Nepali language. Most of the older people do not speak much Nepali language. I translate from English to

> Nepali to Tamang, back in my brain to Nepali then to English. It is challenging when a lot is being said.
>
> I do not translate every word, as some words are hard to translate into exact words. I translate the main messages you are saying. I then listen to the responses and summarise the main points of what the community is saying. If I sense that the community is not quite understanding what we are saying, I will add some more so they understand. Sometimes it just needs to be said in an easier way.
>
> First, we get all the other ideas out and then I may add some. Then we discuss all the ideas, including mine. We decide which ones the majority agree with, and then I translate those back to you. In Tamang culture, mostly everyone needs to agree. It is rare that one of the leaders has a strong view against the prevailing views. When we are talking big issues, there is lots of conversation that narrows the differences in opinion. So villagers with a strong view back off when they hear that conversation or others compromise and move more towards that idea. People must live and work together."

Pratika Shakya, who has a Master's degree in Rural Development, was another good translator, particularly when meeting with local women. She came to Tawal with us as an employee of Joy Foundation Nepal (www.joy.org.np), a Kathmandu-based, non-government social organisation. Joy Foundation Nepal supports several charitable activities, including co-funding an annual remote cataract-surgery eye camp with NAFA. It also provides office administration and other support to NAFA executive members when they are in Nepal and at other times of the year. Although Pratika is from the

Newari caste and therefore does not speak Tamang, we have great respect for her quiet demeanour, ability to listen and competency as a translator. She also understands what NAFA is trying to achieve in the Tawal area. With these challenges and limitations of communication acknowledged, a partnership with the community nevertheless emerged to progress two of the building blocks of development – education and health, the focus of the next two chapters.

Chapter 4

Life experience to formal schooling

Long before a Westerner visited the area, local leaders wanted to improve education in their villages. Before villagers built a temporary school classroom in Tawal and then a small, two-room school at Meledanda, local children helped their parents in agricultural work. Education was informal: taught within the family and gained through life experience. Children learned their culture and practical skills from copying their parents and joining in festivals and ceremonies. They also learned their history through stories and by helping with everyday living tasks, according to their age and capabilities. Villagers had a rich Indigenous knowledge of the local environment, plants, animals, and hunting and farming techniques, as well as a vibrant and ancient culture, passed down orally to the younger generation.

During Rana rule in Nepal, spanning 1846 AD to 1951 AD, Jung Bahadur Rana, the first Rana ruler, started education for his own children within his royal courtyard (Durbar) but opened the Durbar School only to the Rana and his nobles' children. This represents the beginning of modern education in Nepal. The syllabus followed was based mainly on the Indian system, which in turn is the legacy of the British Raj. Durbar School in Kathmandu opened to the public for the first time in 1885.

Before the 1950–51 revolution against direct rule by the Rana dynasty, Nepal had 310 primary and middle schools, eleven high schools, two colleges and one technical school. In the early 1950s, the average literacy rate was 5%. Literacy was 10% among males but less than 1% among females. Only one child in 100 attended school.

Following the revolution, the number of schools increased but lower-caste and ethnic-group discrimination still restricted access to education to relatively few. With poorer families focussing on their livelihoods to survive, most girls and poor children were left out of the education system.

However, in the Tawal area, there was a growing interest amongst villagers in becoming literate and educating local children. The importance placed on education was often sparked by work outside the community. Some men sought employment as porters for the British Army training camp in Pokhara. They took their guests on treks in the Annapurna mountain range, where they met people with high levels of education.

The life chances of one man, Lal Bahadur Tamang, quickened the quest to obtain literacy in the Tawal area. At age sixteen, Lal Bahadur went to an adjoining VDC to do fieldwork for a family, not for money but in exchange for being taught basic literacy skills. He became the first person in the Ree VDC to read and write in the Nepali language. Having a literate person in the Tawal community was a game-changer, providing opportunities for villagers to work together to develop the area in the 1960s.

At just twenty years of age, Lal Bahadur became a political leader in the Ree VDC for the Rastryia Democratic Party. He then devoted his life to helping his community, holding his party position for thirty-five years and using it to advocate for local infrastructure development. Lal Bahadur is still highly respected as the 'village father'; Chandra refers to him as the 'Mayor of the VDC'. At various times, Lal Bahadur travelled to India and to other parts of Nepal to visit relatives and for business. Seeing how people were being educated elsewhere, and the positive impact that was having on their families and communities, motivated him to encourage education in Tawal.

Chandra explained that his father had been similarly influenced by 'outside' work experiences. When Chandra was a small child, his father had travelled to India for work and later to Pokhara to join the army for a short time. He understood how hard it was to earn a sustainable income without an education. Experiencing life outside the village circle seems to be a catalyst for change. But the only primary school in the area was at Rigaun, the administrative centre of the VDC (comprising twenty-five villages), even though Rigaun had a much smaller population than Tawal. This was too long a walk for primary-school students in the Tawal catchment area.

There were also no school resources available in those days. Villagers had to be inventive and use local organic material, as one elder recalled:

> "In the early days, children would use a chalk prepared from the 'simal' tree instead of a pen and a wooden board instead of paper or a writing book."

With no government assistance on the horizon, community leaders decided to act. In 1959, led by Lal Bahadur, villagers in Tawal built a small, temporary school classroom. The first and only teacher at the original school, Dhan Bahadur Tamang, lived in the nearby village of Tawal Besi. He could read and write simple words, which he had learnt from working for someone in Phulkarka, a village in a neighbouring VDC.

A few years later, in 1962, the community built a grass-roofed, two-room school on a hill below Tawal, known locally as Meledanda ('danda' is the Nepali word for 'hill'). The school, which went to

Grade 3 level, was only the second in the VDC. Lal Bahadur was elected president of the inaugural School Management Committee and Chandra's father was also on the committee. The teacher's salary at the time was 90 Nrs (AUD$1.10) a month, paid with funds raised by the community during the annual Dashain/Tihar festival.

Though community leaders knew that education was important for their future, other villagers were not so sure.

> "In those days we were not happy to send our children to school because if they went to school, who would do the household work? But now I have realised that we were wrong. Now I know that if they had studied, they would have become a 'thulo manche' [great person]."

In 1975, primary education was made free and the government became responsible for providing school facilities, teachers and educational materials. Primary schooling was compulsory; it began at age six and lasted five years. Secondary education began at age eleven and lasted another five years in two cycles – two years (lower) and three years (higher).

The school at Meledanda grew, and because he had a Grade 5 education and was therefore considered more qualified, Sun Bahadur Gurung was recruited from Phulkarka to replace Dhan as teacher. Sun's father was from the Tamang caste but had changed his caste name to Gurung for a better chance of recruitment into the British Gurkha Army, then a prized career option for local villagers. While a teacher in Tawal, Sun boarded with Chandra's parents in Tawal. The school at Meledanda was officially recognised by the Nepalese government thirteen years after being built by the community.

A five-room government school was then built on the current school site, above Meledanda. The land was purchased from local farmers through the old Gau Panchayat system and the community helped with construction. Eleven other primary schools in the VDC would eventually be built during the time Lal Bahadur was in his elected position. Other important pieces of community infrastructure, such as suspension bridges, were also built, providing villagers with safe means of crossing rivers and connecting them with markets and services in Dhading Bensi and Kathmandu.

Nowadays, at age seventy-six, Lal Bahadur says that he gains much satisfaction when he looks around and sees "all these things". He feels he "fought for [his] village and [his] area" and had "done many good things". He has a great love of community: "I love this place and it is difficult to leave", although most of his friends have died and many in his family live elsewhere.

Many of the current leaders in the area started their education in the original school at Meledanda. Like other local leaders who followed, Bhim Tamang started his study at Meledanda, then continued his education at a school closer to the district capital, Dhading Bensi. He was the first student from the Ree VDC to sit the national School Leaving Certificate (SLC) exams, considered the 'iron gate' to college in Nepal, at the completion of Grade 10. He went to Dhading Bensi to sit the exams but failed. When Bhim tried again, a year later, he was told that the course content had changed in the past year, and he would have to repeat Grade 10. Of course, he was disappointed, but returned to Tawal to teach at the old school for two years. However, he lost that job when the new school was built, as he did not have teaching qualifications (SLC Certificate) and returned to farming.

But Bhim remained interested in education. Forty-five years later, in February 2019, I symbolically handed the keys of an eight-classroom school to Bhim in the village of Kutal. The school had been destroyed by the Nepal earthquake in April 2015. Bhim was Chairperson of Kutal's School Rebuild Construction Committee. His efforts as a young man had come full circle.

Faising Tamang, Sri Bahadur Tamang, Lok Tamang, Bal Bahadur Tamang, and Dipak Tamang all started their schooling in the old school at Meledanda. They all continued to Grade 5 in the newly built government school at Tawal and then boarded at a village closer to Dhading Bensi for Grades 6 to 10, before returning to become important local leaders.

Faising returned from passing his SLC exams to take up a permanent government teaching-quota position, remaining at Tawal for nine years. He had to leave during the Maoist insurgency and was the first person from the area to go to the Middle East (Qatar), where he worked in the agricultural sector. He returned to become a successful farmer and took on the important volunteer position of Chairperson of the Micro-Hydro Functional Group that oversaw the construction of a 20 kW electricity system (see Chapter 6). In the November 2017 local elections, the first conducted since local bodies were dissolved fifteen years earlier, Faising was elected head of the Ward for the newly formed Ganga Jamuna Rural Municipality.

Sri Bahadur Tamang and Lok Tamang followed similar study pathways to eventually become school principals in Tawal and the nearby village of Latab, respectively. Similarly, Bal Bahadur Tamang eventually became Principal at the school in nearby Dhuseni, and was also elected President of the HRDC.

Like Bhim, Dipak Tamang failed the SLC exams and returned to Kutal, the village he grew up in. Dipak became involved in the issue of freedom of religion. His father was a porter in Pokhara, where he met an American Christian missionary. The missionary gave Dipak's father a Bible translated into Nepali to bring back to the village. He said missionaries from America and Singapore visited the area to 'spread the word' and offer incentives to convert to Christianity, including being supported by the church to attend Christian Bible College in the Terai, near the border with India.

The Panchayat government, led by the royalist party, had declared Nepal a Hindu kingdom, banning conversion to any religion, including Christianity. The police sent letters to Dipak, threatening to arrest him. He fled through the jungle to Gorkha, but others, including Amar Tamang and Bahadur Singh Tamang from Kutal, were arrested. Dipak ended up in the Okhaldhunga district in eastern Nepal, where he began to support the Congress Party, as they championed freedom of religion.

Freedom of religion was subsequently incorporated into the 2007 Interim Constitution and is also enshrined in the new Constitution, promulgated on 20 September 2015. Interestingly, the Constitution does specifically deny the right to convert another person. Dipak's interests were broader than religion. He was an active member of the youth club before it became the HRDC. He would go on to be President of the School Management Committee at Tawal.

However, not all community leaders followed the formal education pathway. Three local builders, Buddha Tamang, Sirap Tamang and Kanchha Dong, had different but equally inspiring stories. Their community and NAFA have relied greatly on them during NAFA's twenty-year partnership with the HRDC in constructing community infrastructure in the Tawal area. They have all earned their respected positions as community leaders through knowledge and skill gained through work experience, initially learning their trade from others, and from years of practice.

Neither Buddha nor Sirap, like many young children at that time, was allowed by their parents to attend school. Their parents said they were needed at home to look after the family's animals. When they reached their teens, they watched men building older-style grass huts, and then, later, watched others build newer-style stone and slate-roofed homes.

Buddha and Sirap built the first two classrooms funded by foreign donors, Guenther and Christa from Austria. They planned and coordinated the construction of the NAFA-funded water infrastructure system in 1999 and the health post in 2000. They told us later that, at the time, their pay was 80 Nrs (AUD$1) a day. They would become the main builders of the school classrooms both before and after the 2015 earthquake, along with construction of the micro-hydro system and agricultural-cooperative infrastructure, the focus of later chapters in this book.

Kanchha Dong also has no formal education or training. Although he wanted to go to school, his parents needed him to look after their goats so would not allow it. Kanchha Dong had six brothers, none of whom was given permission to go to school, but Kanchha taught himself to read and write. For a time, he lived with another man in a house up towards the jungle. He noticed that they could write using a leaf from the 'Bera' (the Tamang word for 'white-coloured') tree. The leaves were good not only for goats and other animals during the dry season, when their more favoured grasses were less plentiful, but also for writing! Kanchha Dong credits Faising for teaching him how to do multiplication. Years later, he would become the manager and tariff collector for the micro-hydro system.

Like Buddha and Sirap, Kanchha Dong learnt how to build through experience gained locally. He learned how to construct concrete pillars for two-storey buildings by being involved in building the first two-storey Christian church in Tawal. He learned electrical work when operating a dynamo for the small ten-house micro-hydro system that preceded the 20 kW micro-hydro system. Kanchha Dong would eventually learn to read government-approved classroom design plans prepared by Sabin Shrestha, a Kathmandu-based architect, after the 2015 earthquake. These plans incorporated earthquake-resistant technical features that represented a major advance from the way classrooms had been built pre-earthquake. Kanchha Dong told us that the earthquake-resistant training NAFA had funded and organised after the 2015 earthquake strengthened his understanding of construction. We deeply admire all three builders – highly competent, honest, hardworking 'can do' people who have achieved so much without the opportunity to attend school.

By 2000, however, the school built with government funds was in poor condition. It was dark inside and the internal walls were damp with mould. When community leaders prepared the Integrated Plan with Lloyd, replacing the old classrooms and extending the school to Grade 10 level were their two highest priorities.

Chandra told us that at that time, most students in the Tawal area, including all girls, stopped their education after Grade 5. Students in the Tawal area who wanted to further their study had to go to villages in another VDC to attend schools in Satobato or Phulkarka which went from Grades 6 to 10. The villages took a whole day to reach if you were carrying goods or four to six hours of 'fast walking'. Chandra says he and his friends could get there in two hours of running!

Only boys were allowed by their parents to go that far to school. Students would leave early on Sunday morning, in time for school's 10 am start. To last the school week, parents gave students an allocation of 600 grams of millet per day, flour and some dried vegetables and/or potatoes. Four or five boys would share a room, the rent representing a significant cost for their families. School finished at 1 pm on Friday, when students would return to their village for their 'weekend'. This was a dangerous journey during the ten-year Maoist insurgency between 1996 and 2006. The Maoists controlled the area, as they did most of rural Nepal, and parents feared their children being kidnapped for recruitment into the Maoist Army.

Just as the Maoist insurgency was ending, an Austrian couple, Guenther and Christa, had raised the funds to replace two of the oldest, darkest classrooms in Tawal. I became President of NAFA in 2007, and another seven new classrooms were rebuilt with NAFA support in 2007 and 2008, bringing the total number of classrooms to nine, including an office for the school principal and the teachers.

Guenther and Christa had subsidised a teacher's salary, which had extended the school at Tawal to Grade 7 level. However, offering Grade 8 and eventually Grades 9 and 10 was not just a matter of constructing classrooms. The Department of Education would approve requests to extend the school beyond Grade 5 only if the community paid the teachers' salaries or were lucky enough to attract foreign support to do so.

For Tawal, this meant subsidising teacher salaries to enable the school to extend initially from Grade 5 to Grade 7, then to Grade 8 in 2005 and finally to Grade 10 a few years later. Five teachers' salaries would need to be sponsored by the community or foreign donors. Extending the school at Tawal was only possible following a visit from Raul Accion, a Spanish air-traffic controller, who came up with us to Tawal in 2008. Recognising the importance of education, Raul offered to sponsor three senior teachers for five years. Together with two work colleagues, Diana Jerez and Alberto del Valle, he set up a small charity in Spain called Smile Back to Me to subsidise the teachers needed. Over the next twelve years, other family members and friends helped make the journey possible, though Raul was always willing to contribute any shortfall from his own pocket. NAFA was now working with two small, like-minded INGOs, Nepaleducaid in Austria, run by Guenther and Christa, and Smile Back to Me, run by Raul with support from Alberto and Diana.

Before heading to Tawal in November 2008, we arrived at Chandra's Kathmandu office to meet Kanchha Tamang, the new teacher to be sponsored by NAFA. Kanchha's position would enable the school to be extended to Grade 8 level. Chandra had referred to Kanchha cryptically as 'small man, but good man'. Seated on the office couch in his white shirt and black jacket, Kanchha looked like a man about to face a job interview. His furrowed brow suggested he was expecting some tough questions! As we introduced ourselves, his face was transformed by a broad smile and perfect teeth. Yes, he was short and slim, and handsome, with thick wavy black hair and even features. He laughed along with us as he tactfully managed to decipher Deb's attempts to speak in Nepali. We knew we would become firm friends, but could not have imagined then how important Kanchha would become as a village leader in the years ahead.

Kanchha was keen to visit a progressive school, so we arranged to meet him at the Bagh Bazaar bus depot to travel to Vinayak Shiksha Niketan (VSN) English Secondary School, a NAFA-supported school located in Thimi, a pottery town about 13 km from Kathmandu. We were to learn that, in defiance of the laws of physics, a bus can never be too full. We started early to make the most of our visit. As we were among the first few on the bus, we felt pleased to find seats near the front, next to the door. The bus heaved its way through the clouds of exhaust from the crawling traffic, taking on an endless stream of passengers at each laborious stop. Windows were shut to avoid the choking fumes, then just as quickly opened to let out the stale air.

Sitting was no more comfortable than standing as the crush of the increasingly overcrowded bus forced people to lean into us, and then on us, as the driver swerved to avoid oncoming traffic, any rules of lane use apparently abandoned. Students' backpacks repeatedly struck our heads! We managed to return their apologetic smiles. Kanchha sat opposite, apparently unperturbed by several small schoolchildren sitting on his lap.

After an hour, we were still nowhere near Thimi. As the bus gathered speed on the four-lane China Road, people were further challenged to stay upright. We feared passengers might start popping out the windows like corks. Incredibly, the bus boy, dangling precariously by a railing outside the doorstep, signalled the driver to stop for a petite, paper-thin woman, bent with age. *Surely, she will wait for the next bus,* we thought. But no, she gave the thicket of passengers blocking the stairs a steely glare and, in one nimble leap, gained a foothold on the first step. As if by magic, she somehow slipped through the crush, emerging triumphant next to the driver. This feat was made even more astonishing by the bamboo basket caging an energetic chicken that she held in one hand and the small goat tightly tethered to the other. The driver's assistant moved to give her half his seat and engaged her in lively conversation. The goat, its front hooves up on the dashboard, had the best view of the road ahead! The chicken now sat quietly, no doubt groggy from the noxious air. On finally exiting the bus, as we walked slowly to allow our bones to settle back into their rightful places, Kanchha remarked nonchalantly, "Bus was very slow today". We all laughed.

More than 500 parents and community members attended a school ceremony organised for our visit to Tawal that year. Chandra and I officially handed over responsibility for looking after the seven new classrooms to the teachers and a student representative from each class. In my speech, I stressed the need for the community to continue lobbying local politicians for more government-paid teachers, whose lack in remote villages like Tawal remained a problem over the next decade.

The HRDC knew that improving the quality of education should not be restricted to Tawal. New classrooms were needed in the feeder schools at Latab, Dhuseni and Kutal. The school at Tawal Bensi, below Tawal, also desperately needed repair. Schools in these villages went to either Grade 3 or Grade 5 level, depending on the size of the village. Students then went on to Tawal for their schooling up to Grade 10. Another school, a two-hour walk away from Tawal, in the village of Richet, also needed new classrooms, though its students by now fed into the other secondary school in the VDC, in Rigaun village.

In 2009, Guenther and Christa increased their support to the Tawal school by sponsoring two teachers, as well as continuing to support a teacher salary at Kutal and at Dhuseni. By January 2010, a multipurpose room had been constructed for the library, computer lab and science lab. A new school toilet block had also been constructed, and classrooms had either been constructed or substantially repaired in the nearby villages of Latab, Kutal, Tawal Bensi and Richet.

However, the level of support to a specific geographic location began to become an issue for some NAFA committee members. Although applying a community development approach requires resources to fund multi-year programs, a few senior members of the management committee felt that the villages benefiting from the community development focus were 'getting too much'. Such disquiet first appeared during the construction of the school toilet block at Tawal.

The project was not a NAFA project, instead initiated and largely funded by two European donors. Guenther (from Nepaleducaid) was an architect and designed the toilets to serve approximately 350 children: three stalls for girls, three for boys, a latrine, and hand-wash basins in each toilet. He sent the plans to an architect in Nepal to ensure they met local building standards.

The HRDC proposed a budget of AUD$6,300, higher than budgets for simpler toilet block designs at smaller village schools NAFA had supported. However, those designs did not include septic tanks. In this case, a toilet block servicing so many students needed a large underground septic tank.

The project then exceeded its budget by approximately 25% because it was discovered that an enormous rock lay beneath the site for the septic tank. The rock would have to be broken down by hand. While villagers contributed some volunteer work, they could not be expected to do so many extra days of excavation without some pay. The extra time involved in breaking up and removing the rock increased the cost of the toilets. I proposed that NAFA contribute a small amount to cover the extra cost.

Concern was expressed in the NAFA committee that the toilet block project cost so much because the design was extravagant, not because of excavation for the septic tank. One committee member referred to the toilet block as 'the Taj Mahal of toilets'. There was a perception by a few committee members that Tawal villagers' requests were 'too greedy'. We discussed these views in committee meetings and reviewed the reasons for the more substantial toilet block and the budget overrun. We believed the issue resolved, but the perception of Tawal 'getting too much' was to re-emerge periodically in the years to come.

Meanwhile, the new classrooms, along with funding of the toilet block by Austrian, Dutch and NAFA donors, made a big difference to school enrolments, especially for girls. Before the new classrooms and toilet block were built, local leaders reported that only 50% of school-age girls in the Tawal area went to school. However, with new classrooms and a new toilet block, the increase in female school attendance was remarkable. In 2012, the first year for which we collected attendance data, girls outnumbered boys by 252 to 186. This was particularly the case in Grades 8 to 10, with girls almost doubling the number of boys. School records also demonstrated how students from nearby villages fed into the 'hub' school. In Grades 6 to 10, 65% of students came from villages other than Tawal.

In response to concerns about students being able to secure their first job following completion of Grade 10, we met with parents in late 2010 to discuss a proposal for NAFA and Smile Back to Me to contribute to the costs of further education and training for up to four students per year who had passed their SLC (Grade 10) exams. The new program, called Further Education and Training (FEAT), would support those students in continuing their study to Grade 11, Grade 12 and then either Bachelor level or an accredited vocational-training course.

Under the proposal, NAFA and Smile Back to Me would contribute on a 50–50 basis towards course fees and accommodation for post-Grade 10 study. The students' parents would fund the rest, which in most cases was about 50% of the total cost.

We hoped students supported for further study would return to the area to work, but we knew this was not a realistic expectation for most students, as there were very few suitable jobs available locally. Before deciding on whether to start the program, we met with parents of the Grade 10 students to hear their views about their children studying in Kathmandu, Dhading Bensi or Pokhara and then perhaps finding work away from their families and village.

The parents accepted that students needed to leave home for further study, and some were already trying to send their children away for higher education but were finding this financially difficult. Parents lamented the limited local opportunities for employment, indicating that many husbands and sons were forced to go overseas for work, especially to Malaysia and the Middle East. But with little education, they were being offered only low-paid and dangerous factory or construction work. Parents said that if children had to go overseas for work, it would be much better to go with some trade skills or higher education so they could secure safer, better-paying jobs.

By 2010, the foundation had been built for improved education in the area. The school at Tawal had been extended to Grade 10 in new classrooms. In 2012, the first cohort of Grade 10 students sat the SLC exams and twenty-five of the twenty-seven students (92.5%) passed (the national 2012 average SLC pass rate was 47%)! Girls outnumbered boys in that class by two to one. Tawal's result was the best of the 150 or so government schools in the Dhading district, a great result for such a remote school.

The first FEAT students supported were Ashok Lama and Kipa Tamang. They completed a six-month electrical wiring course at a government-accredited vocational training centre, the Underprivileged Children's Education Programs (UCEP) at Sano Thimi in the Kathmandu Valley. They would return to Tawal to take up paid positions as operators of the newly installed micro-hydroelectricity system. But before relating the details of that system's construction (see Chapter 6), we will tell the challenging story of funding another key building block for development – health services.

Chapter 5

Faith-healing to blood-testing

In the early years, villagers relied on Indigenous knowledge and practices to deal with illness and injury. Health practices were connected to religious or spiritual beliefs together with plant-based knowledge. Sick or injured villagers sought the help of traditional healers and lamas, who used herb, plant and animal parts for treating illnesses and wounds, as well as spiritual mantras to invoke healing.

> "People would visit 'Chopne Lama' [specialised lama, faith healer] for their treatment. The faith healer would use a mantra to assist the healing. The herbs and shrubs from the forest were used to treat injury."

Herbs were used to treat fevers, diarrhoea and broken bones. A specific grass or moss found on rocks would be made into a paste to assist with treatment of a wound. People also practised animal sacrifice to aid recovery. A frame was used to set broken bones, often leaving the bone misshapen:

> "They would worship God and offer [a] he-goat for their recovery. Wounds or injuries were treated using the extract from herbs and wrapping up the wound with a cloth. If the bone in a hand or leg was fractured, it would be treated by putting the extract from the herbs on the affected area and then putting the hand into a traditional bone-setter made from bamboo. Although this treatment would cure the pain, the bone did not come back as its original shape."

There was a high child-mortality rate before the health post was established.

> "If you ask any elder grandma in this village, you will know that if they had given birth to nine or ten, or eleven, or twelve children, only four or five would survive."

The first two NAFA projects in Tawal were health-related. First was water infrastructure, installed in 1999, bringing water from the Kalsyong Khola to Tawal and two nearby villages, Dhuseni and Serchet. Second was construction of the health post, co-funded by NAFA and AusAid, Kathmandu. The health post began operating in mid-2002, after construction had been delayed during the Maoist insurgency.

In addition to Beg Tamang, a female health worker was needed in the area to focus on women's maternal health. NAFA offered to sponsor training of a second health worker. However, having experienced Nima's tragic death at the completion of her training, the community decided to sponsor the training of two female health workers, with Lila Maya Tamang and Sunita Tamang offering to share the equivalent of one salary. The women completed a nine-month Child Health Worker course, then learned midwifery practice from Beg and through on-the-job experience. We met Lila Maya and Sunita in Chandra's office in November 2005. They seemed shy but friendly and were clearly committed to their study. We gave them some textbooks NAFA had purchased that were compulsory for their course. They expressed their gratitude at being supported for training and work at the health post. Seven years later, in 2012, Sunita enrolled in an eighteen-month (plus six months' practicum) Auxiliary Nursing Medical course at the Lalit Polytechnic Training Institute in Kathmandu. Lila Maya followed in November 2018, when she went to Kathmandu and enrolled in the same course.

The health post at Tawal was not formally registered with the government when it was built. The issue of registration was not considered by the NAFA committee, perhaps because AusAid did not require registration as a condition for their grant. We are not sure why the health post was not registered, as we were not actively involved in NAFA at the time. When asked about it, Chandra says his role was to find a donor and he left registration to local community leaders. It is possible that there was a collective suspicion by the community and by Lloyd of the Nepalese bureaucracy, which has long had a reputation of being politicised, rigid and ineffective. There was concern that government registration would come at the cost of local community control over who would be employed at the health post and how it would operate.

However, the ongoing subsidy of health-worker salaries became an issue within NAFA, especially as allocations increased to support salary increases in line with inflation. The issue, which reflects the complexity of providing community development aid in developing countries, will be discussed again in Chapter 14. In January 2010, I asked the HRDC to investigate the benefits of formally registering the health post, including possible government quotas for health-worker salaries.

In hindsight, should NAFA have pushed harder for registration? Even if it had, would the Nepali government have responded positively? We suspect not. But we also acknowledge that indefinite sponsorship of health-worker salaries (or teacher salaries, for that matter) is not sustainable for a small international-aid agency run entirely by volunteers, even with NAFA's generous and loyal supporters.

When we visited the health post, Beg showed us three sets of books in which patient-related data were recorded: a Daily (Patient) Treatment Book, a Family Planning register and a Government Outback Register. The Daily Treatment Book gave a useful summary of patient data. On average, ten to twelve patients were visiting the health post daily, though the numbers varied greatly according to the season. The busiest time at the health post was the hot monsoon season. Villagers most commonly presented with traumatic injuries and common illnesses – diarrhoeal diseases in the monsoon season and respiratory concerns in the winter. Women commonly suffered from dehydration and exhaustion due to long days working in the fields without adequate fluids, often requiring a saline drip.

All three health workers, particularly Beg, were very good at suturing wounds. Over the years, we witnessed his stitching skills, and heard stories of Beg, Lila Maya and Sunita saving the lives of villagers. One woman was virtually 'scalped' when her hair got caught in a grinding stone run by a water mill. Another man Beg saved had been attacked by a bear in the community forest above the village. We also met a villager who had fallen, hit a rock and sliced his head open from the top of his right ear to the top of his left eyebrow. Beg stitched all of these wounds, without the need for patients to be evacuated to the hospital at Dhading Bensi.

We also met women whose babies were saved during childbirth. At one baby clinic hosted by the health post, Beg introduced a mother and her baby, safely delivered by Lila Maya despite the baby being in a breech position in late pregnancy. Lila Maya was able to turn the baby just before delivery. The mother thanked us for supporting the health post and said she felt she owed her own and her baby's life to the support Lila Maya provided during the difficult birth.

Although the health workers kept a Daily Treatment Book, a card system was not maintained to record a patient's medical history. If health workers needed to check back on previous visits, they needed to go through the Daily Treatment Book or rely on their memory and personal knowledge of the patient.

The Government Outback Register was completed during government inspection visits. Although the health post was not officially registered, the health department in the district headquarters at Dhading Bensi knew of the health post and used it extensively to host outreach visits to the area.

In 2009, an Australian doctor visited Tawal with his family. On inspecting the records at the time, the doctor was impressed with both the data being collected and the treatment being given. He and his family were to become the principal financial supporters for this important primary health service and building block for community development.

In January 2011, community leaders indicated to us that before the health post was built, a mother or newborn baby would die, on average, every six months. Beg confirmed that no mothers or babies had died during childbirth since then. Apparently, two babies had died before 12 months of age, one from cholera and the other from typhoid, though Beg said the reason for the latter death was that the child's parents did not give her the medicine prescribed. While there may be a little luck involved, it is mostly a great credit to Beg, Lila Maya and Sunita's training, skills and experience that the maternal and baby survival rates have improved in the area.

In that same visit in 2011, Beg identified the need to test blood, sputum and stool on-site, so villagers would not have to travel to Dhading Bensi for sugar levels, haemoglobin counts and the diagnosis of typhoid, tuberculosis, diabetes, cholera, STDs, HIV and other diseases. NAFA funded Beg to undertake blood-testing training in Kathmandu, at the end of which his lecturer advised him on the type of microscope and other equipment needed to do blood tests. AusAid, Kathmandu subsequently approved an allocation to purchase a microscope and centrifuge, and Beg's trainer accompanied him to Tawal to help him set up and test the equipment. In August 2011, Beg became the first health worker in the VDC with the skills and equipment for testing blood.

One of the limitations of relatively short visits and not knowing the local language is that our impressions may not represent an accurate picture of the reality. While there seemed to be evidence and community feedback confirming a good level of primary health care at the health post, there did not appear to be an organised general health outreach or preventative health program. Beg told us they did talks at the school on topics such as family planning, HIV and STDs, but this appeared to be only a minor part of their health program. When asked about attempts at health promotion, the health workers would reply unconvincingly that they tried, mainly on an individual basis, but people did not 'take much notice'.

We wanted to explore the issue of health promotion with the villagers to gain their perspective, but this proved challenging. The acknowledged limitations of translation (referred to in Chapter 3) undoubtedly meant a loss of useful insight into health-worker perspectives. We also had no way of knowing how our questions and comments were being interpreted. Were our questions about health promotion interpreted as an implied criticism that the workers were failing to carry out what was to us an important health activity? The conversations also emphasised the role of gender in communication. The female health workers were often quiet in our meetings, leaving Beg to do the talking. Despite being asked direct questions, they would say little and defer to Beg.

All three health workers appeared puzzled by the idea of providing health workshops or school-based health promotion. They were trained to treat common illnesses, stitch wounds, monitor pregnant women, help mothers deliver their babies safely, and support mothers with their new babies. But they had no training in public health education and outreach. Without specialised training, changing entrenched health practices is challenging, even for the most well-resourced health agencies in Western countries, so it was little wonder health promotion was not part of everyday practice for the Tawal health post.

We were still hoping the three health workers would be open to discussion on preventative health-education activities, but they remained hesitant and far from proactive. Our feeling was that our discussion possibly left them feeling inadequate in relation to this aspect of health practice. Was it fair to expect them to have conducted such activities without training? During our January 2011 visit, Beg identified the need for health-education training. It has remained an issue ever since.

In our early visits, Beg also identified the need for other ancillary health services to visit the area and conduct optical, dental, general health and women's health clinics. It would take many years to source the funds and identify opportunities to organise these clinics. An eye clinic was the first such area we explored.

NAFA had been supporting the Kathmandu-based Tilganga Eye Centre (now called the Tilganga Institute of Ophthalmology) since 1991, co-funding an annual cataract-surgery eye camp with a local Kathmandu-based charity, Joy Foundation Nepal. But the Tilganga bus that carried the equipment needed for the camps could go only as far as the end of the bitumen road. In the Dhading district, that was Dhading Bensi, more than a day's walk away from villages in the Tawal area. Villagers would need to wait until an eye camp was planned for Dhading Bensi, then take the long walk to and from district headquarters.

However, an opportunity arose to organise a hearing clinic in the area, thanks to two compassionate ear-care practitioners from Whitsunday Hearing, a hearing service in northern Queensland, Australia. Lew and Sue Tuck were NAFA members, Lew an audiometrist/engineer and Sue an audiologist with thirty years' experience in public hospital and private audiology. They offered to come to Tawal with us and conduct a hearing clinic.

At the time, neither Beg nor other community leaders had raised the need for a hearing clinic. However, that was not surprising. Whereas eye clinics were well known and established in Nepal, ear camps were not. Difficulties experienced by those living with hearing problems in remote communities were accepted as a part of life. Hearing aids were unheard of. Applying a community development framework, it was an example of raising community awareness of a health issue, sharing information about that issue, and leaving it to the community to decide whether members wanted to participate or not. Beg was consulted in Tawal and took responsibility for identifying and registering people with hearing problems.

In January 2010, Sue and Lew came with us to Tawal, the first time an audiologist had visited the area. Over three days, Sue and Lew conducted hearing tests at the Tawal health post, with priority given to over forty villagers identified by Beg as experiencing hearing loss. Nine villagers were fitted with hearing aids donated by Sue and Lew. Four villagers were promised a different style of hearing aid, to come from Australia three months later. Seven spare hearing aids were left at the health post.

Applying the principle that those who could afford it should pay at least a little, each villager receiving a hearing aid paid a 150 Nrs (AUD$1.90) deposit, to be retained by the health post. A token amount (10 Nrs) was also paid for replacement of the batteries Lew and Sue donated to the health post. They trained Beg to perform hearing tests and do basic maintenance on the hearing aids. Expensive technical equipment and hearing-aid batteries, also donated by Lew and Sue, were left at the health post so that Beg could continue to provide basic primary hearing services after Sue and Lew returned to Kathmandu.

The community response to this first-ever hearing clinic was extremely positive. The HRDC could see the need for widespread screening of men, women and children from all villages in the area to identify hearing problems and promote good ear care. They asked for a multi-village hearing clinic the following year and took responsibility for organising it.

The HRDC proved to have superb organising skills. News of the upcoming clinic was spread on radio and by sending a 'kata wal' (town crier) to each village to advise people of the event. The January 2011 hearing camp was conducted by Sue, Lew, and Keshab Man Dangol, an otologist with the Nepal Association of Hard of Hearing (NAHOH), a small, not-for-profit hearing-service NGO based in Kirtipur, near Kathmandu. Ten years later, Keshab was also to play an important role for NAFA after the onset of COVID-19 (see Postscript).

Villagers came from every village in the area and beyond, having heard about the free clinic. Over five days, 509 ear examinations were conducted, including every student at the hub school in Tawal. The families of school students were asked to contribute 10 Nrs for the examination, which Sue and Lew donated to the health post for the purchase of much-needed medicine. Many foreign objects were found in the ears of students, including a piece of wire, a cockroach and other dead insects, sticks, stones, a feather, seeds and straw! More than 100 students with compacted wax needed syringing of their ears. Many students had ear infections and some had perforated ear drums. Those who needed operations were given Keshab's contact details for follow-up in Kathmandu. Sue and Lew fitted eight new hearing aids, and left behind posters on good ear care.

Sue and Lew returned to Tawal with us a third time, in November 2011, for what was to be a six-day combined hearing and eye clinic. Dr Detlev Gueck, a German eye doctor, had been working with Kopan Monastery monks in India and Nepal for many years. He joined the clinic to perform eye examinations, treat infections, and prescribe and fit pre-assembled glasses he brought with him from Germany.

Written invitations for the combined ear and eye clinic were sent out to other villages in the VDC. A community-service announcement on the Dhading Bensi-based FM radio station attracted villagers from other areas, some of whom walked over six hours to the clinic. The combined clinic registered 1,078 people who had their ears checked, then went next door for an eye examination. The specialists worked from dawn until dusk to assess all who came. Dr Gueck fell asleep over his meal one evening, his unending effort having finally got the better of him.

Over the six days, approximately 250 pairs of glasses were issued by Dr Gueck free of charge. Dr Gueck reported a higher incidence of cataracts than he had previously experienced in his camps in Asia and India. He attributed this largely to the smoke from open wood fires used in the homes for cooking. The feasibility of stoves that used less wood and emitted much less smoke into the house was first raised at this clinic. The idea was followed up later through an improved cooking-stove (ICS) program, the focus of Chapter 8. Those villagers requiring cataract surgery would need to go to Kathmandu or wait for a cataract clinic to come to Dhading Bensi.

In the adjoining hearing clinic, fourteen more villagers received hearing aids, including an older gentleman who had walked for over six hours to have his hearing tested. In lieu of the small financial contribution expected towards the cost of aids supplied, he showed his appreciation by singing a song of thanks to everyone present. On this occasion, Sue and Lew felt that his determination to reach the clinic and his joy at receiving a hearing aid were payment enough!

It would be more than five years before oral, general and women's health clinics could be organised for the area. But they would happen. The building blocks for development had been put in place. What was needed now was a stimulus to economic development: access to electricity.

Chapter 6

Turning the lights on

By 2008, we had reached a crossroads with the Tawal community. In accordance with the community development framework, we had begun the process of understanding the context, though we still had much to learn. Relationships with key community leaders were being developed, albeit within the constraints of annual visits to the area. Needs and priorities had been identified, and villagers were now enjoying a village water supply, a basic health-care service in a well-constructed, staffed health post, and rebuilt classrooms and a toilet block at the school. The school had been extended to Grade 10 and new classrooms were being built in nearby 'feeder' schools going either to Grade 3 or Grade 5 level.

At this point, NAFA could have ended the asset building and maintained the more limited option of sponsoring the equivalent of two health workers and two teachers until government funding for those services eventually became available. After all, there were many other villages in Nepal in need of basic health and education facilities who would be thrilled with that level of support. However, the community consultation process of identifying priorities and strategies for change had opened our eyes, and those of the villagers, to several opportunities outside the education and health sectors. It started with a proposal to construct a micro-hydroelectricity system that would provide electricity to the school and the health post, as well as to households and prospective small businesses in the two villages of Tawal and Tawal Bensi.

Assessment of this proposal would be complex, with higher risks than other projects supported to date. Much more community participation would be required in all phases of the project: planning, construction and operation. The project's potential for capacity-building was great, but so were the risks. It was an area of development we knew nothing about and, at first glance, seemed far beyond NAFA's capacity. Should we limit our already significant and much appreciated level of support or delve into the riskier aspects of larger and more complex development priorities? It would be a real test of our collective capacity to apply the community-development framework.

It was during our second visit to Tawal, in November 2008, that access to electricity was raised during discussions with community leaders. For us, it was about the feasibility of bringing electricity to the school and the health post, but for community leaders, it was much more than that: they knew exactly how electricity could transform everyday life.

A small, privately owned micro-hydro system was operating at the time, providing electricity to ten households. Our first thought was that perhaps it could be extended. However, the school and health post were more than a kilometre away from connection to that system and up to two kilometres from the likely site for the power station required by an entirely new system.

When we raised the idea, local HRDC leaders and Chandra expressed the collective view that it would be a waste to bring electricity to the school and health post without connecting power to the 250 households in Tawal and Tawal Bensi villages. The community had long viewed electricity as essential for development and saw this as an opportunity to realise that dream.

During the day, the power could be used by the school and the health post. New small businesses drawing on the electricity supply could provide economic opportunities beyond the existing reliance on subsistence farming. Families would be able to charge their mobile phones and connect their radios to the electricity system. In the evening, the system would provide lighting for the houses.

A solar panel had been installed on the roof of the health post to run the refrigerator and other equipment used for blood-testing and primary ear care. However, solar panels would be more expensive to install for 250 households, school and the health post, as well as being problematic during the cloudy and rainy monsoon season. At the time, the engineers we spoke to in Kathmandu favoured the micro-hydro option. Nepal has a plentiful supply of water, and the small Kalsyong Khola, close to Tawal, had the capacity to provide water to the system all year round.

The planning and implementation of a micro-hydro project would be incredibly challenging for both NAFA and the local community, requiring technical engineering oversight of many months of physical labour from the villagers. Once in operation, the system would need to be managed. As the largest and most complex project ever proposed for NAFA funding, it was outside the comfort zone that prevailed in NAFA at that time and would certainly test NAFA's capacity and willingness to take a calculated funding risk. But the project had the potential to transform the lives of the villagers, who would benefit greatly from access to electricity.

Several factors impact on an assessment of development proposals for donor-agency consideration. The mission of the aid agency and existing project profile are two considerations. Is the proposal consistent with the overall aims of the agency and the type of projects it has funded in the past? In NAFA's case, community development principles were enshrined in its submission to the Australian Government to obtain tax-deductibility status.

However, the NAFA management committee had little experience with adopting a community development approach.

NAFA had up until that point favoured small-scale, one-off infrastructure projects, such as the installation of water taps in a village or school, and a few multi-year health and education projects. A community development approach, on the other hand, compelled a 'big picture', longer-term view of a specific geographic area. This would be a new approach for NAFA, so internal support would need to be tested with the NAFA committee.

Other factors to consider include the agency's experience and willingness to accept risks and capacity to raise funds. Larger projects are typically more complex, riskier to implement and require larger funding allocations than smaller ones. These factors should not be a deterrent but are certainly a consideration. Larger projects can attract new donors supportive of that type of project. But the agency needs to be willing to accept a higher level of risk for projects that potentially can achieve greater change. A risk assessment needs to be undertaken for each project proposal. Finally, the agency needs to consider its capacity to raise funds. NAFA was (and still is) totally volunteer-run and at that time had limited fundraising capacity.

We wanted to 'think big', alongside community leaders. It was an exciting proposal, but one that needed to be tempered by NAFA's limited fundraising capacity and lack of experience with larger, more technical projects. We decided it was time to test the NAFA committee's understanding and willingness to adopt a community development approach.

In March 2009, a presentation to the NAFA committee on adopting a community development framework in the Tawal area was well received, though some reservations remained. At that stage, funding implications were not considered, as the micro-hydro proposal had not been assessed or costed. But we knew there would be challenges ahead when it came to gaining committee support for larger, riskier proposals. We needed to proceed cautiously. We were about to embark on a journey with a very steep learning curve.

In 2009, after receipt of an earmarked contribution from a donor interested in pursuing the project, NAFA agreed to fund a professional engineering consultant to conduct a feasibility study for installing a micro-hydro system, sourcing water from the Kalsyong Khola. We were referred to Suresh Shrestha, Manager of the Rural Energy Development Program (REDP) for the Dhading district. REDP supported the work of the Alternative Energy Promotion Centre (AEPC), established by the Government of Nepal with UN support to promote and implement projects using renewable energy technologies. Suresh would guide the feasibility assessment. If the project went ahead, he would then oversee construction of the system.

In June 2010, a technical report was completed on a 20 kW micro-hydro system to provide electricity for the two villages of Tawal and Tawal Bensi. The report identified several perceived benefits to the community. The system would provide an average 80 watts of electricity per household per day, primarily for lighting, which would improve safety by reducing household accidents after dark as well as allowing for study in the evenings. Families would have an up-front expense to connect to the electricity system. However, on an ongoing basis, even with the payment of a monthly tariff, there would be a projected nett saving for households, as they would spend less on kerosene and dry-cell batteries.

Electricity would bring villagers radio, the main source of news from the outside world, and a handful of households would even have televisions in the future. The one major limitation of the system for households was that rice cookers could not be used, as they would draw too much electricity from the system. That meant households would still need to rely on open wood fires (and eventually on gas) for cooking.

Access to electricity would also enable villagers to expand their economic base by setting up small businesses during the day, such as rural carpentry, welding, a bakery, a tea shop, a beauty parlour and a photocopying shop.

Subject to the availability of funds, the school would be able to install up to ten computers for computer studies, a subject that was by then compulsory for the higher grades. Until then, students could learn the subject only from their textbooks, with no opportunity to practise on an actual computer! There would be lighting for the principal's office/staff room and the multipurpose (library/science lab/computer) classroom, which was also to be used for staff and community meetings.

Micro-hydroelectricity would also be a great asset for the health post. There would be lights for health-care services at night, as well as reliable power for medical equipment, including the microscope, centrifuge and thermostatic water bath used for blood and urine testing, a small refrigerator used for storing medicines and vaccinations, and an autoclave used to sterilise and dry medical instruments.

The total cost of the system was estimated to be 60 lakhs (AUD$75,000). The proposal would attract a Nepali government AEPC/REDP subsidy, sourced from the World Bank, totalling just over 40% (24 lakhs). The community and NAFA were expected to cover the remaining 60% either in cash, in kind or through a bank loan. In addition to technical support, a Social Mobiliser would be funded by the REDP to support the implementation phase of the project. The Social Mobiliser would arrive in Tawal before the estimated eight-month construction project commenced and remain for six months after the power station began operating. His or her role would be to involve the community by organising volunteer labour and linking the community with government programs, thus maximising the opportunities that access to electricity would bring.

The technical report did identify several risks and mitigating strategies. The risks included: possible cost blow-outs during the construction phase; villagers not being willing or able to contribute as proposed in the feasibility report; families being unable to afford the upfront connection costs or the ongoing monthly tariffs; and operators lacking the technical or management skills to run the system once it was operational.

The proposal had both technical and financial risks. Consideration of proposals with such levels of risk was uncharted territory for NAFA committee members. Understandably, several members were quite anxious about committing to the project, despite the mitigating strategies identified in the feasibility report.

While the project had the potential to transform the lives of local villagers, NAFA committee members lacked technical expertise in hydropower. Our first step was to become better informed about the technical aspects of the proposal. Fortunately, a Nepali-born engineer in Brisbane, Kamalayan Shrestha, offered to provide advice on the feasibility report. His experience with hydropower in Nepal before migrating to Australia was invaluable. For over a year, he met with me for lunch in Brisbane's CBD, patiently responding to my queries. He also provided written comments and advice as documentation from the engineers in Nepal regarding the feasibility of the project began arriving. Without Kamalayan's support and encouragement, the project would not have advanced beyond the feasibility assessment phase.

The technical expertise provided by Suresh in Nepal and Kamalayan in Brisbane began to ease NAFA committee concerns about the proposal. Confidence on the technical side was further enhanced when it was agreed that if the project went ahead, NAFA would fund an assistant engineer to act as construction supervisor and oversee the technical side of the project during the construction phase.

Apart from the technical issues, there were concerns about whether the Tawal community really understood the volunteer labour and financial commitments the project would require from them. During the eight-month construction phase, villagers would need to contribute their volunteer labour as an in-kind contribution equal to approximately 20% of the overall cost of the scheme.

Volunteer labour would be needed to porter construction materials such as cement, reinforcement bars, gates and valves, pipes, powerhouse equipment, cables, wires, the generator and the transformer from the road head to the project site. Villagers would have to break up the stones required to make aggregate for concreting. They would also have to source, collect, and carry locally available construction materials (such as sand, stones and timber) for holding tanks, construction of the power station, and supply and installation of the electricity poles.

When construction of the electricity system was completed, households and small businesses would be required to pay an upfront connection fee to cover the cost of bringing the electricity line to the house or small business and installing a meter to record electricity usage. Each household and small business would also pay a monthly tariff, depending on electricity usage. Small businesses would pay more. The monthly tariffs would be set at the level needed to cover the salaries of two operators and a business manager/tariff collector, as well as the costs of repairs and maintenance. NAFA made it clear that the system would need to sustain itself following the construction phase. This also meant that some of the monthly tariff would have to be set aside for the eventual replacement of power-station equipment, holding tanks, pipes and electricity poles.

But despite assurances by Chandra and local leaders that the community would provide the volunteer labour and financial contributions required, debate continued within the NAFA committee. As one member of the committee said at the time:

> "We don't want to find out that the whole thing has fallen into the river".

For some members, a dramatic image such as the system lying in the river at the bottom of the mountain increased anxiety and uncertainty about the project. There were examples of failed micro-hydro projects in Nepal. For example, we had seen one sitting idle in the Solu Khumbu district when trekking in that area. Aid work always has an element of risk, and NAFA relies on the local community to implement and manage every project it funds.

Fortunately, there were a few NAFA donors who heard about the project and had the vision and compassion to believe that the anticipated benefits of the project outweighed the risks. One donor had worked extensively in the field of health in Southeast Asia and had seen firsthand the benefits of electricity to villages. She talked extensively with us about risk management and felt satisfied that the project had every chance of success. The other donor, when asked if he was still willing to donate even without any guarantees of success, replied:

> "Well, what is the worst that can happen? If no-one dies or loses an arm or a leg, it's worth the risk."

Anxieties within the NAFA committee eased somewhat when these two NAFA donors collectively offered to shoulder most of the financial risk for constructing the electricity system. At NAFA's October 2010 meeting, the committee considered a draft Memorandum of Understanding (MOU) involving NAFA, the HRDC and REDP. The MOU provided details of the respective contributions to the project of government, NAFA and the local community. The community's contribution included their in-kind labour, the cost of household connection to the system and the monthly tariff. There was also explicit reference to a base level of electricity entitlement per household, above which they would need to pay an additional tariff.

The MOU confirmed that stonemasons and carpenters would be paid at a negotiated rate, taking "into consideration the volunteer labour that others in the community are providing, so the wage rate may not be the full market rate". A Micro Hydro Functional Group (MHFG) would be established by the community to oversee the project. It would select the electrical and mechanical equipment supplier, coordinate volunteer labour, supervise construction of the system, set the connection fee and monthly tariff, select the two micro-hydro operators and the business manager, and develop policies and rules for use of the electricity. An assistant engineer with technical expertise in micro-hydropower construction would be contracted for the project's estimated eight-month construction phase.

The MOU also stated that NAFA and government funds could be used by the MHFG to purchase safety equipment, including hats, safety boots, gloves and safety glasses, for labourers directly involved in project work such as stonework and pipe works. A volunteer Workplace Health and Safety Officer, nominated from the community, would be given basic health and safety training. They would then promote workplace health and safety messages, and supervise the day-to-day implementation of these messages on the construction site. NAFA and government funds could also be used to restock the basic first-aid kit and equipment at the Tawal health post, to ensure it was adequate for emergency medical aid during the construction phase.

At this point, those of us on the NAFA committee who had steadfastly supported the project were excited but also felt an overwhelming sense of responsibility. We knew the community wanted electricity, which had the potential to transform their lives, but did they have the capacity to implement the project successfully?

There was a lot at stake. We had met with village leaders to discuss the proposal, but had not had the opportunity to see for ourselves how well the whole community understood their responsibilities and whether they were making a truly informed decision about their involvement. I decided to make an unscheduled trip to Nepal to meet with the REDP Engineer (Suresh), then visit Tawal to meet with local villagers. The draft MOU and the Technical Report would form the basis for those meetings.

I prepared a summary of the key information from the Technical Report, including the costs and the community contributions expected of villagers. The summary was translated into Nepali for distribution and discussion with community leaders. The introduction to the summary stated:

> "NAFA, as a possible financial partner of the micro-hydro system, believes it is important that the HRDC and the whole community of Tawal are fully aware of the information that the engineering consultant has

> prepared. The success of this large project depends on community understanding of that information, and agreement to the community commitments detailed in the Report."

I also developed a list of ten questions which I would ask community leaders and the community to ensure they had a full understanding of the project and were giving informed consent to what was being proposed. In November 2010, I met with Suresh in Kathmandu. He reassured us of the scheme's viability and confirmed that it had been successfully implemented in many villages in Nepal.

I then travelled to Tawal to meet with local leaders and villagers. A community meeting was arranged in the central town square. On the day of the meeting, the square was packed with villagers of all ages, sitting and standing wherever they could find a space. There was an air of expectation and excitement, coupled with genuine interest to understand the details of the proposal. Women in Tamang dress and older men wearing their traditional 'pagari' (headscarves) sat quietly in anticipation, waiting for the meeting to begin.

Catching a smile from individuals as I looked around, I knew in my heart, even before I spoke, that they would do everything in their power to make electricity a reality. With the help of a translator who spoke both Nepali and Tamang, I outlined key features of the proposal, including the economic, educational and other benefits to households and small businesses. The crowd listened intently, without speaking. While I waited for the translator to relay this information, I looked around the crowd, and could see villagers nodding as different points were made.

I then focussed on NAFA's expectations regarding community contributions to the project. I told community members that they would need to contribute local volunteer labour and material totalling approximately 20% of the total project cost. I also explained how much it was likely to cost households to connect to the electricity system and then to operate the system once constructed.

There would be a minimum monthly tariff for lights, plus extra tariffs based on additional electricity usage. There would also be a limit to the appliances households could connect to electricity during peak hours, due to the limited capacity of the 20 kW system. The priority would be lighting. Rice cookers could not be used.

I was also very clear about the amount NAFA could contribute towards the construction phase, and the fact that the community would need to cover any construction overruns. I explained that once the system was operational, maintenance and equipment replacement costs would also have to be met by villagers, through payment of their monthly tariffs.

I then raised the issue of equitable access to the electricity scheme. The community was asked what they would do if some of the poorer households were unable to afford the upfront connection fee. In response, community leaders indicated that they would ensure everyone would be able to connect. If poorer families were not able to pay the connection fee, they could do extra volunteer labour or have the connection fee paid by other families in exchange for bartered labour.

Questions were then put to the community to test their understanding of the proposal. Did they understand the features and limitations of the electricity scheme? Did they know what community contributions were expected of them, both during and after the construction phase? I then stopped and waited for the community response.

Conversations started up in the crowd and between community members and the translator. After some time, the translator began to pass on the comments being made. He said the community wanted to reassure me that they fully understood the proposal and the commitments they would be making to the project. They said that they appreciated NAFA's proposed contribution and understood the limitations of that contribution. They indicated their belief that the scheme was critical to the future of their villages, and confirmed they would do whatever was necessary to ensure successful implementation of the project.

To further test their commitment, I asked community members if they would be willing to collectively raise some cash over the following month, to provide an initial deposit towards any cost overruns during construction. The funds would be deposited into the HRDC account. If not needed, they would be returned to the community after completion of the construction phase.

The community agreed at the meeting to raise approximately 1.5 lakhs (AUD$1,875) and deposit this into the HRDC account in Kathmandu by 14 December 2010. The community further agreed that if cost overruns exceeded 1.5 lakhs, they would contribute whatever funds were needed to complete construction. They would need to set up a register whereby each household would agree to contribute their share of the potential construction budget overrun deposit and undertake the volunteer work detailed in the Technical Report.

It had taken two years since the project was first proposed and then assessed. My report on this visit to Tawal reassured NAFA committee members that villagers were committed to making the contributions expected of them, and that mitigating strategies, including the provision of technical support during the construction phase, were in place to reduce potential risks.

In the end, we had to trust the capacity and determination of the community to construct a micro-hydropower scheme with the potential to transform the lives of local villagers. An allocation of approximately 25% towards the estimated cost of constructing the system was approved by the NAFA committee in November 2010. Together with a community eager to make their contribution, the project was underway!

When I returned to Nepal and Tawal two months later, fourteen local community organisations had been established to coordinate and undertake volunteer labour for the project – seven male and seven female groups. Each group comprised approximately fifteen households. Buddha Tamang and Faising Tamang had been elected by the community to oversee the project at a local level.

Our next visit was in November 2011. When following the pipeline from the intake to the holding tanks, we came across a steep cliff area equipped with bamboo scaffolding for volunteers to climb up and secure the water pipes. It looked precarious, and I queried who would be undertaking such risky work.

> "We will send older men up for that job."
>
> "Why?" I asked.
>
> "If they fall, they have had a good life, whereas young men still have a life to live", was the response.

Seeing the look of horror on my face, they quickly added reassuringly:

> "And older men are more careful than younger men!"

While inspecting the construction of the holding tank, high above the power station, we met two young women, crimson-faced from exertion, each carrying 45 kg bags of sand they had collected from the river (a four-hour round trip). Without a hint of irritation, they carefully swung the loads off their backs to look up at us and smile broadly. As they went on their way, we felt humbled by their positive attitude and by their sheer physical capacity to manage such loads over the steep and difficult terrain. This was true commitment.

Soon after, we witnessed another example of the community's positivity, collective strength and sheer determination to succeed. We were with a small group near the power station, waiting for sixteen men to arrive. Eight men on each side were shouldering stout bamboo poles with a 320 kg turbine slung between. It was the end of a three-day trek from the road head at Chimchook, across the valley from Tawal. Over the rise they came (photo on front cover of this book), sweating profusely. Rubber thongs flew from their feet and off the track as they struggled to retain their balance with such a heavy load on what was no more than a goat track. The men negotiated the last few terraces down to the power-station site, carefully placing the turbine on a newly constructed cement pad. We learned that they had completed a similar effort the previous week, carrying the 320 kg generator from the road head to the site.

I suggested to Suresh (the REDP engineer) that it might have been easier to pay a helicopter to bring in the system's two heaviest pieces of equipment. His reply reflected the principle of community ownership:

> "No, it is better that they carry it in. They will then look after the equipment, as they will know what hardship it takes to carry it if that equipment has to be brought back out for repairs."

It was an emotional scene to witness. Although exhausted, the men were cheerful, exuding a sense of satisfaction and accomplishment.

They watched intently as the engineer and electrician assembled the system. We could only imagine the physical strength, coordination and cooperation it had taken to carry such heavy loads up and down these steep, narrow mountain tracks. It was a perfect example of the Tamang approach: creative problem-solving and working together to achieve the desired development-related outcome.

We met with Ashok Tamang, who had received NAFA support to complete a six month electrical wiring course at Underprivileged Children's Educational Programs (UCEP) in Sano Thimi, near Kathmandu. He had also just completed twenty-two days of REDP-sponsored micro-hydro operator training and helped install the turbine outside the power station. The second operator, Kipa Tamang, was scheduled to attend the next training course. Santa Tamang, the system's first Business Manager/Tariff Collector, would soon start eleven days of business training, covering topics including budgeting and bookkeeping.

In February 2012, I was invited by the local community to be Chief Guest and officially open the micro-hydro system. Also present at the official opening were the REDP engineer (Suresh Shrestha), who oversaw the project for the Nepalese Government, the Social Mobiliser (Sunita Shrestha), who helped organise the voluntary labour for construction, a technician from the installation company, a politician from the Nepali Congress party, and two journalists (one from a Dhading Bensi television station and the other from a national newspaper).

I visited the site from intake through to the powerhouse, where I 'cut the ribbon' before being shown the equipment and instruments inside. I then opened the water valve that turned the turbine, which started producing that day's electricity for 250 households in Tawal and Tawal Bensi. Opening the valve reminded me of my father, who had opened many valves in his career as a power engineer. Tears welled as I thought to myself:

> "Dad would enjoy this moment if he were alive and would want to be here with me for it."

What made me even more emotional were the memories of the look of pride on the faces of those in the community who had made the project happen: the women who had carried 45 kg bags of sand up from the river; the men who had walked three days from the road head to the site carrying the 320 kg turbine, and did the same with the 320 kg generator; and Ashok who, having done six months' training in Kathmandu to be one of the operators, had helped the engineers put the machinery together in the power station.

Every family had made significant volunteer contributions to the project, with each carrying an allocated weight of building materials (sand, stones, cement, wire, wooden poles, pipes, and electrical and mechanical equipment). They also had to contribute hours of volunteer labour to undertake other work when requested, such as digging channels for the pipes that transported water from the river to the power station.

Nearly 250 households now had electricity for lights that helped children do their homework during the evening and allowed villagers to move safely around their small two- to three-room homes. Three households who could not afford the connection fee but could manage the monthly tariff were connected 'free of charge'. Electricity would be connected to the school, which could then set up a computer lab, exposing students to the world of information technology. The health post would also be linked to electricity.

REDP engineer Suresh presented a financial summary of the project's construction phase in front of the entire village. He said that all invoices from outsiders (for materials, transport and so on) had been paid and the only wages paid from the project budget were to the experienced tradesmen ('mistris') and their helpers. As there were enough funds in the account to cover all construction costs, the community decided to release the 1.7 lakhs (AUD$2,125) from the HRDC account and deposit the money in the local Micro-Hydro Functional Group account, for any future emergencies.

During his speech at the opening ceremony, Suresh noted that construction of 20 kW electricity systems often took two to three years and usually ran more than 100% over-budget, due to problems at the community level with volunteer labour, local expertise and corruption. Suresh saw it as a great credit to the Tawal community that they completed the project in accordance with the projected timeline and budget.

At that early stage, applications had been received from three small businesses (a furniture-maker, a grain mill and a small poultry farm) requesting connection to electricity. Others would follow, including a baker, a welder, a beauty parlour and an internet/photocopier shop. Years later, using the furniture-maker, Jus Bahadur Tamang, as an example, Kanchha explained that access to electricity had not only changed everyone's day-to-day life but had been life-changing in far more profound ways.

> "Jus Bahadur went to the Gulf country for work but was not successful. He came back and his business attempts failed. He had loans from 'rich' people, paying 24% compound interest. After three years, his loan doubled. He also had no land. But he had skills. He got an idea when the micro-hydro project was being developed. He thought of starting a furniture business. He helped with the construction, doing his share of volunteer

> work. He has done well in his business. He has paid back his loans and has bought some land. He makes windows, beds, cupboards etc., and sells to villages all over the VDC."

Suresh also informed us during the opening ceremony visit that the micro-hydro system was one of five micro-hydro systems in the Dhading district to have been connected to the World Bank Clean Development Mechanism carbon-trading scheme (part of the Kyoto Protocol). For this, the Nepali government would receive some money from the UN to fund other micro-hydro projects. The community was also expected to benefit from this to the tune of approximately 15,000 to 20,000 Nrs (AUD$188 to $250) per annum but never did receive any of the promised climate-change credits.

Before I spoke as Chief Guest, I asked Chandra quietly if it would be okay to say something about the lack of government support observed in the area prior to implementation of this project.

"Say whatever you think is best, Rod."

When Suresh finished his speech, the lead builder for the project, Buddha, presented me with a Certificate of Appreciation in my position as President of NAFA.

Having been given the green light by Chandra, I started by thanking Suresh for his support during the system's assessment and construction stages and by congratulating the community. I then told the crowd, including the government politician in the front row of invited guests, that apart from World Bank funding linked to the new micro-hydro system, I had seen no evidence of new government investment in the area over the seven years I had been coming there. I encouraged the politician, who had brought a large bag of lollies to hand out to the children, to advocate more for villages in the area when he returned to Dhading Bensi, where the district government offices were based.

At the conclusion of the speeches, everyone locked elbows and, in a big circle, danced the traditional Mendho Maya Tamang dance. It was a proud and joyous occasion. Dancing in a circle allows you to see one another, and whenever I made eye contact with villagers, there were smiles and looks of pride, as if to say:

> "Yes, we did it!"

And the children enjoyed the lollies!

That evening, the Dhading Bensi-based politician came to an HRDC meeting that I had requested to discuss a few matters before I returned to Kathmandu. He admitted that what I had said at the opening ceremony was correct, and that like other political parties in Nepal, his party had problems with corruption and indifference towards remote villages. He said he wished things were different, pledging to try and advocate for change when he returned to Dhading Bensi, but there was a sense that nothing would disrupt the status quo.

There undoubtedly would be challenges ahead. But that is the nature of development and change. This community saw electricity as essential for development and worked extremely hard to make it happen. In the Technical Report, the consultant stated that:

> "This project can be a milestone for the starting of other social projects. Since the communities have been mobilized to work in the project environment, it will be easier to launch other projects in the village."

We felt privileged and proud to be part of a small international aid agency committed to working alongside people to achieve their vision of a better life. The collective skills and experience gained by the community through the micro-hydro project would provide the basis and confidence to commence new community-wide projects a few years later, including the establishment of an agricultural cooperative and savings bank.

Chapter 7

Pathway out of poverty

Local villagers in this area had started out as hunters and gatherers before transitioning to subsistence farming. Hunting and foraging for food in the jungle required intense cooperation from all group members to obtain enough food to feed their families. Survival depended on everyone working together and sharing what they procured, such as meat from the animals they hunted. So, the seeds of cooperation amongst local villagers were sown long ago.

As far back as 2001, approximately sixty farmers established an informal cooperative to purchase and plant 24,000 mulberry saplings. Silk farming was Lloyd's idea. He and Chandra visited Khotasi, a large silk factory near Kathmandu. Bhim Tamang, a farmer from the nearby village of Salleri, agreed to drive the initiative locally. Mulberry trees were common in the area. Leaves from the tree were fed to the goats, and the children liked the berries.

There was a large silk program in the district, and an agricultural expert from a district government office was consulted about the proposal. Bhim was offered training at a farm where many mulberry trees had been planted. It was Bhim's first attempt at crop diversification. However, as is often the case with the introduction of new crops, the project proved more complex than first envisaged. Harvesting was quite complicated, and good storage boxes were needed. In addition, buyers were interested only in higher-volume supplies.

Unfortunately, on top of these harvesting and marketing issues, the agricultural expert had neglected to warn local farmers that monkeys also love mulberries. Monkeys waited in the nearby forests until the mulberry trees were a few feet tall, then sent out raiding parties to feast on them. Monkeys stripped saplings of every leaf in their search for the prized berries. As the monkeys had no intention of leaving the area any time soon, the fledgling trial of this higher-value crop was abandoned, along with the dream of a local silk-farming industry.

Following the mulberry tree debacle, other farmers experimented individually with different crops. Faising Tamang planted tea trees, but much of his initial crop died, being unsuitable at the altitude planted. However, he learned from that experience and subsequently planted more successful crops higher up.

An innovative farmer from Dhuseni, Balsing Tamang, planted a few coffee trees, and these did much better. He was to become the leading risk-taker in the local agricultural sector. Like the three leading builders in the area (Buddha, Sirap and Kanchha), Balsing had not been allowed to go to school. He taught himself to read and write and learnt his farming practices from agricultural technicians, word of mouth, magazines, and a weekly national radio program on agricultural cooperatives.

Tall with short-cropped hair and a wide smile, Balsing is a reserved man who observes and takes his time before speaking. During one of our visits to the area, Balsing took us and a few other cooperative members on a tour of his coffee and cardamom terraces. Back at his cottage, he asked if we would like to try the honey from the hives on his cottage roof. Thinking a few spoonfuls of honey would help boost our energy after a long, hot walk, we nodded, but should have known Tamang hospitality did not stop at just a few spoonfuls of anything. We each received a large bowl of honey, complete with a sizeable chunk of honeycomb and several buzzing bees! This was complemented by a cup of coffee made from coffee beans Balsing had grown himself and roasted in a pan over a traditional stove. Over the next hour, we valiantly consumed what seemed like half our body weight in honey. We declined sugar in our many cups of coffee.

Balsing experimented with different crops, learning by trial and error. Believing too many local farmers were growing millet and corn, which were not cash crops, he set a goal of bringing in one or two lakhs (AUD$1,250 to $2,500) per year from cash crops. His first crop was garlic, but garlic was not used in making one of the local staples, 'dhindo', a millet flour and water mix. His parents pressured him not to grow any crops they could not eat but he ignored their advice, as his yield from the garlic crop was five times that of other crops he had grown on that piece of land.

However, after a while, his garlic was not selling. It was too small for the restaurants, which preferred the much larger Chinese garlic, so Balsing changed to growing onions, which were being brought into the area. But each season he found that the onions rapidly deteriorated while being stored. So he started growing coffee and cardamom.

We became interested in assessing the economic status of villagers in the Tawal area, and in March 2011, Deb conducted a survey of income sources to gain a better understanding of the local economy. A total of thirty farming households in Tawal participated in the survey, which provided valuable information on the local context for economic development as well as an insight into the future.

Apart from Balsing and a few other local farmers, villagers in the Tawal area were primarily subsistence farmers, producing for local consumption. None of the surveyed households reported sales of agricultural products or livestock outside the village. Farmers indicated that they traded or bartered agricultural products, animals, kerosene and labour with other villagers to survive.

The primary source of cash income was the production of cane baskets ('dokos'), used everywhere in Nepal to carry goods. It was seasonal work, fitted into spare time from agricultural work or in the evening after working in the fields during the day. Agents purchased the dokos at the end of the road head (up to two hours' walk one-way), with the price based on the size of the doko. Before the doko was made, bamboo had to be collected from the community forest, cut and washed. An average of two dokos could be made in a day, and 50% of those surveyed indicated that they earned an estimated annual income of 6,000 to 11,760 Nrs (AUD$85 to $168) from the sale of cane baskets. It was supplemental income at best, not enough to support the family but rather used to buy or barter for such basics as food and kerosene.

The bamboo that grows in the area is of high quality. However, its availability was becoming an issue, with villagers having to go further into the forest to collect it. The road was being extended, each year coming closer to the area. Villagers indicated in the survey that they hoped to diversify, growing crops such as coffee and selling more products to outside markets. They also identified furniture-making and small poultry farming as possible ventures when electricity became available.

Villagers had long before identified the need to diversify their crops and improve animal husbandry and knew how to work together to make this happen. Balsing also believed the consciousness of local villagers was changing.

> "They now accept that some areas are better than other areas. For example, cardamom and coffee are best grown in this area and can be exchanged for rice grown in the Terai. Each village gets a different amount of sun, soil and water availability.

> People also used to only eat dhindo and curry. Now villagers realise it would be healthier to eat different food."

Balsing knew he needed training in growing coffee and cardamom but could not arrange this for himself. He had his own private nursery and had planted 1,000 coffee plants, but there was a limit to the quantities he could grow on his own. His solution was to collaborate with others in a cooperative arrangement, accessing training and combining with others to sell bigger quantities of crops to outside markets. Most importantly, Balsing was willing to share his knowledge and experience with others.

During the construction of the micro-hydro system, farmers from local villages met informally to discuss the possibility of a more systematic and collective approach to farming. They knew that access to electricity could help provide new opportunities for them. Kanchha later told us it was their experience of collectively constructing and managing the micro-hydro system that gave local leaders the confidence to seriously consider the feasibility of establishing an agricultural cooperative and savings bank.

Apart from Balsing, Kanchha Tamang was the other driving force in establishing the Cooperative. Kanchha had studied cooperatives as part of his Bachelor of Business Studies. When he completed his degree, he was asked to apply for the position of Marketing Manager with the Royal Gorkha Cooperative Savings Bank, set up for retired Gorkha soldiers. However, after due consideration, and with Chandra's encouragement, he instead decided to return home to Tawal and become a social studies teacher at the school, with his salary funded by NAFA. A few years later, he was elected President of the HRDC. He later told us that when he returned to Tawal, he had tried to convince local farmers to invest in establishing a cooperative, but they were reticent.

In 2013, after many local meetings with prospective household shareholders, an application was submitted to the district office of the Department of Cooperatives in Dhading Bensi, with thirty-seven founding members. The application was successful, and a certificate was issued, approving the establishment of the Pasang Chowk Agricultural Cooperative and Savings Bank. Kanchha was elected President of the Cooperative, while Balsing, the largest investor, became the Cooperative's first Treasurer.

Together with Balsing, Kanchha provided the overall vision for the Cooperative. His tertiary study and serious, accountability-focussed nature would ensure that all government regulations regarding cooperatives were met, particularly in relation to accurate record keeping. Ramesh Tamang, a senior mathematics teacher at the school and senior lama at the monastery, became the volunteer bookkeeper for the Cooperative. Like Balsing and Kanchha, he was respected and trusted in the community. Within a relatively short period, 200 households from four villages had joined the Cooperative.

We could not have been more delighted when told, during our visit to the area in November 2013, about the establishment of the Cooperative. Building on improved educational and health outcomes, together with access to electricity, the Cooperative provided the potential for a realistic pathway out of poverty for villagers within its catchment area.

Soon after the Cooperative was established, Balsing identified 25 'ropani' (1.25 hectares) of land above the village of Dhuseni, in a good location not far from Tawal. The Cooperative purchased the land and volunteers built a stone wall around the boundary of the property. Cooperative leaders arranged for an expert from the agricultural office in Dhading Bensi to visit the area, test soil conditions, measure the various altitudes of this very hilly region of Nepal, assess the availability of water and provide advice on crops suitable for the area.

Cooperative leaders followed that advice. They visited other areas of Nepal known for producing high-yield new cash crops or higher-yield animals. They visited Palpa and Saigaun to evaluate coffee, cardamom and goats, and Chitwan for chickens and goats. They considered trialling Kiwi fruit but decided against this because of the need to distribute the fruit to market very quickly after it was picked. The road head was two hours' walk away at that time, and the very rough road from there to the district capital of Dhading Besi was open only part of the year, outside the monsoon season. Chickens were the venture decided upon.

Two chicken sheds, one for broiler chickens, the other for egg-laying chickens, along with a caretaker's cottage and the stone boundary wall, were constructed at a cost of 25 lakhs (AUD$31,250), using funds provided in the initial capitalisation of the Cooperative by its founding members. A caretaker, Som Ram Tamang from the village of Dhuseni, was employed to look after the Cooperative land and manage the broiler and egg-laying chicken businesses that were to be the main income-earners for the Cooperative in the early years. Chicken meat was soon being supplied to nearby villages, with three people being paid to distribute the chickens. A year later, eggs were also being sold to villagers.

During our November 2014 visit to Nepal, we were keen to know how the Cooperative was progressing. In Kathmandu, we met with a technical officer from the National Tea and Coffee Development Board central office. He confirmed that the Dhading district was one of five areas in Nepal where good-quality coffee was being produced. In Tawal, we met with Balsing, who discussed his vision for the future of coffee-growing. We decided to follow up a lead from Chandra about a major coffee-grower from the same district. With Balsing, we visited the Himalaya On Top Organic Coffee Estate near Dhading Bensi, then met with its Managing Director, Bharat Raj Regmi, in Kathmandu.

At the time, Bharat was one of the largest coffee growers in Nepal. He was committed to supporting local coffee growers, with 100,000 coffee plants now growing in his local area. He told us he sold his own coffee beans to Scandinavian buyers and mixed coffee beans purchased from other local farmers to a buyer in Germany. In the preceding year, he had also supplied, at low cost, 8,000 nursery-size coffee plants to the district agricultural office, to help local farmers begin growing coffee beans. This visit inspired Balsing to expand his production and reinforced our collective belief that coffee was a viable and potentially profitable crop in the area.

The Pasang Chowk Agricultural Cooperative Savings Bank was established, operating as a local, farmer-owned credit union, encouraging savings and providing loans to Cooperative members. The Nepal Department of Cooperatives sets the interest rate paid to depositors (12%). Money is collected every fifteen days from Cooperative members in Tawal, Tawal Bensi, Latab and Dhuseni. After twelve months of operation, there were 400 depositors (230 families) in the Savings Bank, with nett bank balances totalling nine lakhs (AUD$11,250), an average of 2,250 Nrs (AUD$28.10) per depositor. This modest level of collective savings began to increase steadily over the next few years.

In response to the demand, Savings Bank deposits were, from the beginning, immediately loaned out to a waiting list of Cooperative members. A villager must be a member of the Cooperative to obtain a loan.

Kanchha estimated that 80% of loans from the Savings Bank were lent at the government-set interest rate of 18% for small-business ventures, education and other purposes such as house building, with the remaining 20% lent at the government-set rate of 15% for agricultural purposes. These interest rates compare to the 24% charged by private moneylenders in the community.

Bank loans had also been available at a lower interest rate of 13% to 14% but required significant paperwork and had to be secured with land titles, based on the land/house valuation. Kanchha said that villagers were wary of the bank loans.

> "A few villagers lost their land and house when they couldn't make their monthly payments on their bank loans, and others were frightened by that possibility."

The Cooperative Board approves borrowers. Once a borrower is approved, their loan application is then assessed and approved by the Loan Mobiliser Committee, which comprises two teachers and another community member. Members can borrow up to 100% more than their savings balance in the Savings Bank, to a maximum loan of two lakhs (AU$2,500). If the loan request is greater than one lakh (AUD$1,250), a land title has to be offered by the borrower as collateral. With the two lakhs limit, many Cooperative members still had to borrow from other moneylenders at 24%.

Borrowers sign a Memorandum of Understanding (MOU) for the loan approved by the Savings Bank. Interest is paid every four months, and if the loan is not fully repaid within a year, a new MOU must be signed. As no cash is kept at the Cooperative, members wanting to make withdrawals must wait until one of the loans is repaid or more deposits are made. When a withdrawal is requested, loan applications are held back for approval and the depositor wanting to withdraw funds is given priority.

The 3% to 6% difference between the interest paid on deposits and the interest received on loans is intended to cover the costs of operating the Savings Bank, as well as making a small profit for the Savings Bank and its shareholders (Cooperative members). Savings Bank expenses include a small salary and commission paid to the person collecting deposits from individual Savings Bank passbook holders, as well as collecting debt interest and repayments from those with loans. This usually involves early starts, before daybreak, in order to visit depositors and borrowers living in villages up to an hour away before farmers leave home to tend their fields and animals.

In the months before our November 2014 visit to Nepal, I spent many hours planning two management training sessions for members of the Cooperative, adapting a framework and notes from the UN Habitat Local Elected Leadership Training Program. Notes for the workshops were written in plain English, then translated into Nepali by Nepal-born NAFA supporters in Brisbane.

In preparing for the training sessions, I first thought a structured agenda would work best. The agenda would cover important management issues that I felt members of the Cooperative would undoubtedly come across as a member-owned organisation. But on arriving in Tawal, I reflected on the principles embedded in the community development framework. I wanted to adopt a process that would encourage participation, with the aim of strengthening local capacity. I knew that discussion needed to start at the Cooperative members' base level of understanding and focus on topics of most interest to them. I decided that it was better for members to identify what issues were important to them and start the discussion with those.

Twenty-one members of the Cooperative attended the sessions, including eleven members of the Cooperative Board. In the first training session, I asked those attending to identify management issues that could determine the success or failure of the Cooperative. The list that was prepared formed the basis for discussion over two training sessions conducted on consecutive days.

Those attending the workshop emphasised the importance of ensuring that the make-up of the Cooperative Board was representative of the local community. The board would comprise thirteen members, with representatives from across the catchment area: women, low-caste (Hindu) Dalit families (more on these families in Chapter 19) and young farmers. Cooperative members also acknowledged that responsibilities associated with developing and running the Cooperative needed to be shared amongst the members. They wanted to discuss ideas to promote sustainability by building capacity within the Board and membership through mentoring, training and sharing administration tasks. Ironically, we would be having the same conversation concerning sustainability and succession planning within the NAFA management committee four years later!

Cooperative members identified the need to develop a business plan and a set of written policies and procedures. They stressed the importance of preparing agendas, practising good meeting procedures, keeping minutes of meetings, handling complaints, and dispute resolution. Transparency in financial record-keeping, and good rules for managing risks such as bad debts in the Savings Bank, were also identified as administrative tasks critical to the future success of the Cooperative.

In the workshops, a few Cooperative members indicated they had been invited to attend training at the Government Cooperative offices in Dhading Bensi and Chitwan. They identified the need for on-site training on a range of agricultural-related matters but said they lacked the funds within the Cooperative to bring in the specialist trainers. Two of their members, Nabin Tamang and Santa Tamang, attended training on managing cooperatives and accounting organised by the Cooperative Office. However, more training was needed.

I was impressed by their interest in management matters. Some of these issues had no doubt arisen in managing the locally based HRDC and the micro-hydro project. Other issues would arise over time. By the end of the training, I felt that the Cooperative was on a slow but steady path towards growth and sustainability, without outside help at that stage. How could anyone know that just six months later, their world would be in turmoil and their dreams of higher-earning, sustainable farming shattered? But before we come to that, another health-critical, labour-saving, environmental initiative was to be introduced to the area: improved cooking stoves.

Chapter 8

Less smoke, no more coughs

Deforestation had long been a problem identified by Chandra and local leaders in the Tawal area. It is, of course, a worldwide issue. Here, they knew full well that deforestation increased the risk of landslides, especially during the monsoon months (June to September).

Deforestation was also increasing the time taken to gather wood for cooking purposes. Locally, wood was taken from both privately owned land and government-owned 'community forests' for cooking with traditional tripod-style 'stoves': a round metal ring on three metal legs. Families, mostly women and children but also grandparents, often took up to eight hours or more to collect wood and return home, sometimes two or three times a week. The extra time taken to collect wood meant lost productivity – less time in the fields, making dokos or studying. There were also safety concerns, especially if older people were caught in the forest overnight, unable to reach home due to deteriorating weather conditions or lack of light.

But perhaps an even more significant health hazard, again especially affecting women and children, was cooking on the traditional stoves. It is estimated that women and often children spend at least two and up to seven hours per day cooking. Without chimneys, smoke from these stoves posed a threat to the health of those cooking, as well as to the environment.

A community development process was commenced in 2012 to create a multi-strategy plan for sustainable forest use. The plan involved: trialling improved cooking stoves (ICSs); developing, in conjunction with Department of Forestry officers in the district capital of Dhading Bensi, a Community Forest Management Plan (CFMP) for the area; establishing a nursery to propagate deep- and shallow-rooted trees; and reforestation on both public and private land.

The first step to be implemented was the piloting of ICSs. A NAFA member, David Brown, visited Nepal in March 2012, and while there went with Chandra to the Centre for Rural Technologies (CRT), meeting with the CRT Director, Hari Gopal Gorkhali. They looked at one- and two-pot 'rocket stoves', suitable for villagers in lower altitudes, and metal stoves designed for villagers at higher altitude. Use of the stoves would reduce the wood needed for cooking by up to 50% and the smoke emitted when cooking inside by over 80%.

In November 2012, we met with Mr Gorkhali at CRT in Kathmandu to gather the information needed to prepare a proposal for introducing ICSs to the Ree VDC. In this case, we would be bringing new information regarding a possible strategy to address an issue they had identified. However, in accordance with community development principles, local villagers would need to be fully consulted, own the process for assessing the feasibility of trialling ICSs in the area, and agree on any proposed implementation of the trial.

Prior to our visit to Tawal, the HRDC sent out written invitations to other villages in the VDC. The HRDC also sent around the 'kata wal' (town crier), who went from village to village 'announcing' the upcoming meeting to discuss the ICS proposal and inviting villagers to attend. The meeting was held shortly after our arrival. Over 300 villagers from more than ten villages attended the meeting; unsurprisingly, the vast majority were women. Attendance reflected the strong collective belief that a practical strategy was needed to address the growing issue of deforestation.

We used whiteboard drawings and a translator proficient in the local Tamang language to explain the ICS proposal and seek initial feedback. At the same meeting, villagers also expressed interest in establishing a nursery to facilitate reforestation, acknowledging that current use of the government-owned 'community' forests was unsustainable. Initial feedback on the ICS proposal was positive. An 'expression of interest' list subsequently completed at village level contained nearly 500 names from an estimated census total of 1,100 families in the Ree VDC, comprising twenty-five villages. Most families expressed interest in the two-pot rocket stoves.

Four months later, representatives from nine villages travelled to CRT in Kathmandu to learn about the ICSs and decide which type of stove to trial. They preferred the low-altitude rocket stoves that incorporated metallic combustion chambers embedded within a housing made of local materials. They felt the alternative all-metal stoves would be too hot in the summer months.

On the way back to Kathmandu, we stopped in Dhading Bensi and met again with district Forestry Department officers, who outlined their CFMP. They explained that as a first step, each village would need to identify which community forest they accessed and each family would then need to sign a village agreement to 'protect, develop and utilise' that forest.

Each village would then submit an official application to the district Forestry Department, which would be assessed. A technician would be sent to the area, at community/NAFA expense, to conduct an Initial Environment Assessment survey, which is a 'resource inventory' of the community forest related to that community.

A Community Forestry User Group would then be set up to prepare the CFMP, which would include data on existing forest stock. A district ranger would guide the work carried out under the CFMP, meet with the community, and develop a detailed Reforestation Plan.

The Reforestation Plan would indicate the capacity of the community forest to sustain a population, including a stocktake of the existing trees and an assessment of how many more trees of which varieties needed to be planted. It would also include a proposal to establish and run a local nursery and an offer to provide subsidised seedlings for the nursery.

If the application for support was successful, the Department of Forestry would establish the program, provide training and technical support, help establish a nursery and provide the seedlings. Departmental staff indicated that the model had succeeded in other villages, so the Forestry Director invited village leaders to visit them and see for themselves.

Of course, the proposed plan was not straightforward. The first step, identifying which community forest each village accessed, proved difficult. Different villages shared common community forests. For example, villagers from Tawal, Latab and Dhuseni use the Pasang Chowk community forest for wood collection. Villagers from Kutal, Richet and Salleri go to nearby 'jungle' or collect wood from their own land. They do not use Pasang Chowk for firewood, as it is too far for them to travel, but do cut large timber there for house building.

In August 2013, CRT submitted a proposal to NAFA for the training of installers and the piloting of the two-pot rocket stove in the Ree VDC. Extracts from the proposal highlight the problem Nepal has with village reliance on wood for cooking (or, in the higher altitudes, yak dung, which is even more of a health risk to women):

> "More than 85% of total energy demand in Nepal, primarily for cooking and heating purposes, is met through biomass (primarily yak dung) energy, and more than 90% of total energy demand of [the] rural population is met entirely through the combustion of fuel wood in traditional (tripod-style) stoves... The traditional approach to biomass burning is often inefficient, which results in production of bulky amounts of harmful pollutants such as carbon monoxide, particulate matters, nitrogen dioxide and sulphur dioxide, with severe health implications."

An initial trial of seventy two-pot stoves was proposed. Housing for the stoves would be constructed from locally available materials, including mud and rice husks. Inside the housing, the design of the stove incorporated a metallic chamber 5.5 mm thick, into which pieces of wood were fed for burning. A metallic chimney took the smoke out of the house. A seven-day training program conducted by CRT staff would instruct nominated installers from participating villages to construct the housing for the stoves. Participants would also be trained in maintenance and made aware of the health and environment benefits of reducing indoor smoke.

Families would contribute towards the cost of the stove housing, metallic chamber, stove top and installation. They would also pick up their CRT stove parts at the end of the road head. NAFA would contribute to the stove parts and pay for the transport to the end of the road head. The total cost of each stove, including installation, was to be 2,214 Nrs (AUD$27.68), nett of a Nepali government subsidy. Families would pay 800 Nrs (36% of the total cost), with NAFA donating the remaining 64%. More than 500 villagers signed a register indicating interest in purchasing low-altitude stoves and paid a deposit towards the stoves. The first seventy ICSs were ordered in August 2013.

In November 2013, training was conducted by two CRT staff, including the lead trainer, Mr Damodar Karki. Fourteen nominated installers (all men) from different villages attended the training program. NAFA had encouraged the nomination of female installers but no women asked to take part in the training. Women were invited to a workshop session on the benefits and use of the ICS, but the numbers attending were lower than expected, as local women were busy harvesting millet at the time. This was an acknowledged problem in applying our community development framework to trialling the introduction of the stoves. Women were going to be the primary beneficiaries of the initiative yet were mostly absent from the training program, except for one community awareness-raising session. This was inadequate, and in hindsight, we should have drawn on the relationships we had developed to insist on higher levels of participation and ownership from local women.

Over the next twelve months, the stoves were installed in six villages. Feedback from villagers indicated that the fire-gate (through which wood was fed into the combustion chamber) was a little too small for easy lighting of the stove. An order of seventy more stoves was made in March 2014, this time with larger fire-gates. However, due to harvesting demands and the fact that some trainers had gone overseas to work, only thirty-four units of the second order had been installed by the end of October 2014.

In early November 2014, Mr Karki returned for a follow-up visit to the area. As the training program mainly involved the male installers, Mr Karki recommended a second community awareness-raising program for women about the benefits and operation of the ICS.

He proposed that the awareness training also include kitchen management, regular maintenance, and the cleaning of cooking pots and the kitchen generally.

Mr Karki also advised using smaller pieces of bamboo ('nigalo') to help ignite the stove, heat up the metal combustion chamber and speed up the cooking process. To increase the rate of installation, Mr Karki recommended that further incentives be offered to the installers to engage in promotion activities and to become full-time rather than part-time installers. It was later suggested that installers be paid more per stove installation to encourage the roll-out of the ICSs at a faster rate.

When we visited Tawal later that month, Deb coordinated an evaluation of the ICS initiative, an important component of the community development process. Thirty-five villagers were surveyed in eight villages. The survey found that 57% of the respondents used the ICS exclusively, with 43% indicating that they also used the traditional tripod stove on some occasions, such as for cooking food when they had guests or if cooking food for cattle. Villagers in the higher-altitude villages also reported using the open-air (tripod) stove for winter warmth.

Those surveyed reported that the ICS reduced wood use by between 30% and 50%. They also reported improved cooking efficiency, better health status, improved safety and an improved household environment. All respondents said that they had changed the way they cooked after using the ICS. Those who elaborated on these changes referred to being able to cook two items at once and, after stopping to feed wood into the stove, having enough heat for further cooking or boiling water without adding more wood.

Importantly, respondents reported significant health benefits.

> "It [ICS] produces less smoke and reduces breathing problems."
>
> "Less smoke … no problems with breathing."
>
> "Less smoke, no more coughs."

The following table summarises the survey results on changes in health status following ICS introduction:

Health problem	No change	Improved a little	Improved a lot	Problem gone	Total for individual problems
Headache	-	9	12	9	30
Irritated eyes	-	10	7	9	26
Bad cough	-	10	4	12	26
Difficulty breathing	-	6	5	14	25
Sore throat	-	8	6	7	21
Chest pain	-	6	4	8	18
Totals for all problems	-	49	38	59	146

The data on health outcomes were encouraging. Responses indicated that all health issues had improved, and in many cases, smoke-related health problems had disappeared.

> "When we used the old stove, because of the smoke, we had eye irritation, throat problem and difficulty breathing. But after using the new stove we don't have these problems anymore."
>
> 'It is stopping breathing problem, cough and eye problem."

> "Because of the ICS, my health is improving and there is less chance of suffering from long-term problems."

> "No more problems in breathing, eye irritation and no headache. Don't have any problem breathing due to less smoke."

Lighting the fire and heating up the combustion chamber remained an issue, even with the larger fire-gates incorporated in the design of the second order of ICSs. Other problems identified during the evaluation included a perception that extra maintenance was required to look after the stoves and difficulties with cooking dhindo, a local staple of water and millet flour, which required the use of large pots and lots of stirring.

Some villagers were also experiencing problems with the chimney in windy weather.

> "At first the wind blew the smoke back inside, but that has now been fixed with a tin cap."

Three respondents mentioned that the ICS was safer for mothers and their children:

> "Safe for children because other parts not hot and only iron getting warm, so daughter can touch without hurting."

> "While working in the kitchen, there is less chance of burning hands or any other parts of [the] body."

> "It stops getting burned and dark spots [on pots]."

The following table of survey results regarding the impact on household cleanliness of the change to using ICSs was also encouraging.

Extent to which household problems from smoke improved

Household Problem	No change	Improved a little	Improved a lot	No longer a problem
Smoke in house	-	2	9	14
Black walls	-	2	12	8
Dust in house	-	2	8	12
Ash in clothes	-	2	8	15

By January 2015, ninety ICSs had been installed, though quality-control problems were being reported with the second batch of stoves. This time, locals noticed that some metallic chambers were thinner than ordered and were melting when heated. CRT promised to replace the faulty chambers. In a local awareness-raising strategy, community leaders offered to provide training to women in their respective villages on how to use and clean their ICS. It seemed that despite some problems being experienced, the initiative was progressively proceeding as planned.

But what was certainly not in the plan was the impact of a natural disaster just four months later!

Chapter 9

The day their world changed forever

On Saturday 25 April 2015, life began as it had for more than 300 years. It was the weekly day off for more than 400 children attending the Tawal hub school. Villagers were in their fields, tending maize and millet crops. Children too young to be in the fields were in their slate-roofed homes being cared for by their grandparents.

Then, at 11.56 am, a 7.8-magnitude earthquake struck, changing the world forever for villagers in this area and so many others in Nepal. The epicentre was approximately 25 km to the west at Barpak, in the Gorkha district. Kanchha and his wife, Lala, were cutting bamboo on their land above the village. Their three-year-old daughter, Rinchhen, was with Kanchha's parents in a temporary shelter, also above the village. He will never forget the moment the earthquake struck and the chaos that followed.

> "The sound was deafening – first a loud rumbling like a bomb, then the horrible sound of collapsing slate and stone from the roof and walls of our houses. Large rocks rolled down from nearby hills. We were beside a big rock, and jumped behind it as rocks tumbled down the slope in landslides triggered by the earthquake."

Kanchha and Lala were close enough to the village to witness the horrific sight of houses being reduced to rubble as aftershocks struck, each lasting about a minute. Their first reaction was one of shock, fear and overwhelming concern for the rest of their family. Were

Rinchhen and her grandparents ok? They ran, screaming, trying to unite with their family. On the way, they met Kanchha's father. They had managed to get out of their shelter just before it collapsed, and he was rushing up the hill to see if Kanchha and Lala were safe.

In a house in the village, Radika Tamang and Santi Tamang were not so fortunate. These two friends, both in Grade 9, had earned 150 Nrs (AUD$1.88) pocket money loading their dokos with goods at the end of the road head, bound for the local shop in Tawal. They were resting from their four-hour round trip when the earthquake struck. While others ran or crawled on all fours for open spaces, Radika and Santi hid under their bed, as they had been taught to do in school. The Nepalese Government earthquake procedures were based on the experience of well-built houses in Japan, where the major risk was from items falling off the walls, bedside tables and cupboards.

Hours later, when the aftershocks finally began to subside, people returned to their collapsed houses to see if everyone was accounted for. A neighbour could hear one of the girls calling for help. When the stones were dug out, Radika was still alive, but her friend had been fatally injured when the house collapsed. Radika asked for a drink of water, which she sipped before dying in her neighbour's arms. The pocket money was found in the girls' pockets.

> "Many in the village were injured, with broken bones and cuts. Before communication was cut, we phoned the district office, and after four or five hours, an army helicopter arrived in the area. Ten army men were let down by rope, and they prepared the helicopter pad near Gamrong, above Salleri. Smaller helicopters landed on the crop fields in Dhuseni the day after the earthquake and picked up six injured people. Community members decided who was most severely injured."

Lok Tamang was at home when the earthquake struck.

> "I would have died in the earthquake if it had happened during the night, as the top floor, where our bed is, collapsed onto the ground floor. I stood under the door frame as the house shook, then I ran outside as our house started to collapse. My wife and daughter were attending a wedding in Pokhara, and our other two daughters were on their way to the wedding. We were all separated, which was very frightening. I walked for seven days to be reunited with my family."

Reflecting later, Kanchha agreed with Lok, Chandra and others that over 90% of the local villagers, including his family, would have been killed if the earthquake had struck at night.

> "Many rocks covered my bed in my destroyed house. We were lucky that way. There are two opinions in the community about the timing of the earthquake. The younger generation thinks it was good luck. The old generation think it was good karma that brought the earthquake during the day off. If [it was] bad karma, the earthquake would have happened at night."

Mobile telecommunications with the outside world ceased not long after the earthquake. If you had your mobile in your pocket when the earthquake struck, you had coverage for the rest of the day, but batteries soon ran out of charge, and with the micro-hydro system badly damaged by the earthquake, villagers were unable to recharge their phones. Emergency medical care was desperately needed, but though helicopters flew overhead, poor weather conditions and lack of communication with those on the ground meant they could not land.

A harrowing story sent to us by messenger brought home the despair villagers were experiencing. Mika Gole, one of NAFA's sponsored students, was studying in Kathmandu at the time of the earthquake. She learned by mobile phone how three of her family members perished in her village of Kutal. Responding to Deborah's text to all the students to find out if they were safe, she told us the devastating story.

> "Thank you for your help and love. I am fine but I am sad. In that earthquake I lost my small sister and grandfather and grandmother. The earthquake destroyed our house – we lost everything. My parents and other five sisters are safe in the village but there is no food to eat, no water to drink and no clothes to wear. My family are living under the open sky in the jungle. Five days passed but the government is not there to help them, so I am in tragedy."

Two weeks passed and somehow Mika, along with several other young NAFA-sponsored students, managed to make the dangerous journey on foot across landslide areas and blocked paths to reach Kutal and Tawal. Nothing could have prepared Mika for what she saw when she was reunited with her family.

> "My mother – her head is broken [large open head wound]. When I met my parents and sisters I could not control myself looking at my mother's condition and my broken house."

Lila Maya and Beg were doing all they could to treat Mika's mother's injuries, but as her condition was not considered as life-threatening as others, she had not been evacuated on the first helicopter rescue flights. Finally, after two nightmare weeks of fearing the worst, Mika and her mother were flown by army helicopter to the field hospital in Dhading Bensi, and then later to Kathmandu for CT scans and surgery. Mika's family lost rosy-cheeked and chubby-faced two-year-old Rajel and both grandparents. The trauma of that terrible time was still raw when we shared a cup of tea with Mika's mother in their makeshift shelter six months later. She told us she has a metal plate in her head and sometimes experiences headaches. She feels grateful to be alive but her heart aches for her youngest child and her parents.

Three NAFA-sponsored health workers from the Tawal health post were in different locations when the earthquake struck. The Coordinator, Beg, was in a jeep on his way back to the area, after visiting his wife and children in Kathmandu. With the road blocked by a landslide, Beg returned to the district hospital at Dhading Bensi, which was overwhelmed with earthquake victims. Next day, he travelled back to his home village of Kutal to attend to the injured. Eighteen villagers, including eight of Beg's relatives, died in Kutal on the day of the earthquake.

Health worker Sunita, on her day off, was at home in the nearby village of Salleri. Like Beg, she was prevented by landslides from reaching the Tawal health post, so she remained in Salleri, treating earthquake victims. That left Lila Maya as the sole health worker for the four villages of Tawal, Tawal Bensi, Dhuseni and Latab. Lila Maya was at church when the earthquake struck. She grabbed the small medical bag she always carried, which contained medicine she might need for house calls at night, and managed to make it back to the irreparably damaged health post, salvaging any other medicine she could. It would be a traumatic, exhausting week ahead.

Lila Maya did not sleep that first night and had little sleep the following week. She visited each of the four villages, treating earthquake victims, including fifteen gravely injured villagers who were eventually evacuated by army helicopter. One of those she helped was Tarsya Tamang. After receiving the call for urgent help, Lila Maya trekked an hour up to Latab through what was then a very landslide-prone area. She found Tarsya unconscious with a big gash to her leg. She stitched the gash, as well as a cut on Tarsya's daughter Mitsang's leg. Lila Maya administered a drip for Tarsya and stayed up all night, then left medicine and trekked back down to Tawal to tend to other earthquake victims.

When helicopters could finally land, they picked up seriously injured earthquake victims: three from Tawal, seven from Dhuseni, and twelve from Latab, including Tarsya. Villagers estimate that around 150 people were evacuated from Tawal and nearby villages to hospitals in Dhading Bensi and Kathmandu.

Médecins sans Frontières (Doctors without Borders) sent helicopters to the schoolgrounds at Tawal, bringing tents, plastic sheets, blankets, soap, gloves, hammers and nails. When their first helicopter landed, Kanchha recalls a staff member speaking to the grateful crowd of villagers.

> "We are bringing this aid directly to you, as we fear that if we gave it to your government, you would not receive it."

Villagers later recalled the turmoil, the chaos, and the struggle for immediate survival that included dealing with physical injuries. They were in shock, unable to think, walking around in a daze. It took a few days for community leaders to collectively adopt a more systematic approach to surviving the immediate impact of the earthquake. They needed to search for food and set up temporary shelters in areas they hoped were safe from further landslides.

One villager said his wife was crushed by their fallen house.

> "We could only see her head."

She was dug out but had sustained multiple injuries, including leg, hand and rib fractures, as well as spinal damage. The villagers carried her to and from the schoolgrounds, seeing helicopters flying overhead, but for several days, rain prevented the helicopters from landing.

Finally, a helicopter was able to land, and she was taken to a hospital in Kathmandu. Her husband was not allowed to accompany her, but when their son begged to go, the pilot relented. Her husband recalled how he felt, being separated from his wife and not knowing if she would live or die.

> "I didn't know what was going on for one month – I just cried and walked around."

Luckily, she survived, and years later showed us all her x-rays from the ordeal.

Another couple we spoke to lost everything. They wiped away tears as we talked, saying they had lost their grandchild, Santi Maya, one of two Tawal students who died in the earthquake. The grandmother, milking their buffalo nearby, saw their house collapsing. The grandfather said he fainted from the shock of the earthquake and could not remember any details. They said they had had no food for days and only dirty water to drink.

> "We had to drink water normally given to our goat and water we had kept for the toilet. After three or four days, people got more organised and dug out food from the rubble of their houses. After five days the helicopters dropped bags of beaten [flattened] rice, but all split upon impact and only 45 packets of 'chow-chow' [dried noodles] were not damaged. We broke those packets up and gave [them] to the smallest children.

> After one month some NGOs arrived with food, tents, and pots and pans. Then NAFA's roofing tin and rice arrived by helicopter – which helped a lot. As a community, we all tried to gather what we could – working together really helped. Family members helped one another, and everyone shared what they had. Because we had lost a grandchild, people even gave us extra food and help."

A seventy-five-year-old widow told of how she was on her own in the field. She could see the houses collapsing and the dust rising. She went to her cousin's place and they stood together, holding hands, crying and screaming. Being on her own, she said, she had no-one to help her. All her food was lost in the earthquake and her two goats were killed. She moved to where she could access water. She was hungry for seven days, then other villagers gave her food. She stayed with her friend for a month – during that time, she said, she felt "really lost". But, "now I am okay. I was given a tent and then the roofing iron." Six months later, all her possessions remained under her collapsed house.

Another older couple lost a son-in-law and grandchild in Kutal.

> "The wrong people died", one said to us. "I am old and can't do anything and I am still alive. Now I am living near the landslide-prone area – if it wants to take me, take me. I am too old. It is my time to go. I wish God had taken me."

They have made sure their grandchildren are now living away from the landslide-prone area.

> "If it comes again, they will be safe."

Mobile communication was finally restored for one of the mobile networks, and a solar charger was salvaged from the local Buddhist monastery, enabling villagers to recharge their phones. Photos began to be sent out, showing devastating damage to the area. Some outside NGOs responded in varying degrees to the immediate needs of the area. The welfare arm of the Kadoorie Charitable Foundation (British Gurkhas) provided packets of immediate aid items. United Mission Nepal and the Red Cross supplied bags of rice. After Médecins sans Frontières, several other medical teams arrived, all without notice, some teams arriving more than a month after the first earthquake struck, long after the injured had been airlifted to hospital.

Locals later recalled that apart from Médecins sans Frontières, the most useful medical team was one organised by the Non-Resident Nepalese Association who, although in Tawal for only one day, gave the Tawal health workers some medicine for the upcoming monsoon season. Conditions in the cluster of temporary shelters that had been set up were refugee camp-like, and one of the doctors in the group was so concerned that he left 50,000 Nrs to construct a community toilet.

Other medical teams had good intentions but were not so helpful. One team of heart specialists went away disappointed because there did not seem to be any heart-related traumas that could be treated. Nevertheless, the help received in the first few weeks was very much appreciated by those to whom we spoke. The help from the Nepalese Army helicopters evacuating seriously injured earthquake victims was especially appreciated. Practical help from organisations such as Médecins sans Frontières was also particularly welcome. But everyone to whom we spoke was disappointed that no government officers came to assess the damage or help coordinate the initial disaster response.

Altogether, seventy-eight villagers in the Ree VDC died in the earthquake, including eighteen from one village and sixteen from each of two other villages. The death toll included a teacher from Kichet, a village high above Tawal. He had been hired from outside the village and supplied with a house for his accommodation there. For him, instead of a day outside tending fields, Saturday was the day he washed clothes, prepared for the upcoming school week and rested. He died inside.

With the epicentre of this very powerful earthquake located only 25 km west of Tawal, every structure in the area, except for a couple of toilet blocks built by the Gurkha welfare association, was destroyed. Having never used iron rods, cement or other earthquake-resistant building techniques in the past, villagers in the Tawal area literally watched their entire world crumble before their eyes. In addition to the terrible loss of life, all 1,225 homes were destroyed in the twenty-five villages. Villagers lost most of their local infrastructure, including schools. In Tawal, the hub school for six villages, built by NAFA and our partners, was destroyed. The health post lay in ruins, including its toilet block, flattened by a big boulder that had tumbled down from the hill above.

The power station for the 20 kW micro-hydro system was also severely damaged, including the instrument panels. Luckily, the turbine and generator remained intact. Elsewhere in the system, most poles and lines were down. Other NAFA-funded infrastructure that was damaged or destroyed included the pipes that brought water to taps in Tawal and 140 improved cooking stoves in collapsed houses.

In addition to infrastructure built with outside funds, villagers also lost assets in which they had invested through the Pasang Chowk Agricultural Cooperative: a caretaker cottage and two chicken sheds lay in ruins. On the day of the earthquake, there were 700 chickens. When the earthquake struck, the caretaker ran down to Dhuseni to be with his wife. He returned next day to find that 300 of the chickens had died when the walls collapsed and the roof came down. On the first night after the earthquake, a further 100 chickens were eaten by jackals who had come down from the forest. The surviving 300 chickens were either sold by the Cooperative or distributed to Cooperative members.

The monsoon season was fast approaching, and more landslides were inevitable. Outside help with shelter and food was desperately needed.

Chapter 10

You are all living in an ivory tower

When the earthquake struck, our family was in Tokyo, attending a wedding. Our daughter Angela was the first to see on the internet that an earthquake had struck Nepal. News regarding the epicentre was slow to reach us in Japan, which has little English-language television. We celebrated our nephew Morgan's joyous wedding to Aya on Sunday, but our thoughts were also in Nepal.

As we flew back to Australia the next day, our worst fears were realised. The epicentre was near the area to which we had travelled so often in the past ten years. When Qantas news confirmed the extent of the damage caused by the 'Gorkha earthquake', tears flowed. We were devastated.

We arrived home from Japan late on the morning of 27 April, two days after the earthquake. Awaiting us was a slew of emails, and an urgent request to join leaders of Brisbane's Nepalese community, who were meeting that night to plan a response to the earthquake. At that stage, we did not know how NAFA could or should respond. But everyone knew the need would be great.

Nepal-born NAFA members in Brisbane asked me for NAFA's support in meeting the urgent needs of victims. A few members of the Nepalese community were agreeable to raising funds for NAFA but wanted a say in, or even the right to decide, how money was to be allocated in Nepal. Others argued that some of the funds raised should be donated to the newly established Prime Minister's Fund in Nepal, set up to collect donations from home and abroad. Different views were also being expressed, both within the Nepalese community and later within NAFA, on how funds raised in Queensland should be spent. With emotions so high, it was not surprising that a range of views was being expressed.

An important point made at that meeting helped focus our planning. One of the doctors in the group had phoned colleagues in Nepal, who told him that clothing was flooding in, as were some medicines, but these items could already be supplied from within Nepal. People in different parts of the country needed other types of help. The doctor advised the group to listen to the people in Nepal, not assume we knew what they needed. We heeded that advice, which was consistent with good community development practice: let those affected identify their needs and priorities, then negotiate solutions, taking into consideration the funds available.

Donations were starting to flow in from the Nepalese community, NAFA's broader support network and the general public wanting to help a country in dire need. We waited for communication from our contacts in Nepal. An email arrived from Kanchha in Tawal, via Chandra in Kathmandu, a week after the earthquake. It identified roofing tin and rice as the most urgent requirements for survival through the fast-approaching monsoon season.

Villages had set up emergency shelters in areas they felt were safe from landslides triggered by the earthquake and its aftershocks. However, the makeshift shelters, set up with whatever could be salvaged from the earthquake rubble, were inadequate for the heavy monsoon rains. Food also lay underneath the debris, either inaccessible or destroyed by the rains that accompanied the earthquake. A new crop of millet was about to be planted, but there was an immediate need for a staple food like rice.

> "Food had been stored in the house but had got mixed with clay and rocks in the earthquake. Even if found, a few weeks after being dug out, the food was spoiled and could not be eaten."

After the chaos that followed the immediate aftermath of the earthquake, local leaders began to meet and prepare a request letter for outside help. They conducted a quick survey of households in the Ree VDC: the total was 1,225 households across twenty-five villages.

> "We considered the VDC as one whole family. Everyone faced the same problem after the earthquake. So, we asked for help to everyone in the VDC. We were not sure if NAFA and other donors could help in such a large way, but we thought we should try."

The request letter, sent by mobile phone to Chandra in Kathmandu, requested 1.5 bundles (twelve sheets) of eight-foot (2.4 metres) long, colour-bonded, corrugated-iron roofing per family for temporary shelter and 60 kg of rice to sustain villagers until crops could be planted and harvested. Chandra knew someone working in an investment bank who did business with Hulas Steel Industries Limited, the largest roofing-tin manufacturer in Nepal. That contact got us in the door and secured a reasonable price for the roofing tin during a time of extraordinarily high demand.

Hulas provided Chandra with a quote to manufacture the roofing tin, and the cost of 60 kg (two bags) of rice per household was added to the proposal. The budget for 1,225 households totalled 11,345 Nrs (AUD$141.80) per household, nearly 140 lakhs (AUD$175,000) overall. At the time, this figure seemed unattainable for a small, volunteer-run aid agency and the like-minded donors in Spain and Austria we knew would also want to help.

After doing the maths, I spoke to Chandra by phone.

> "'Chandra, the HRDC request is so big! I don't think we can raise that much money in such a short period of time. Couldn't we commit to purchasing roofing sheets and rice for the five villages NAFA has supported in the past?"

Tamang people are known for their sense of fairness, and Chandra's response expressed this in a very practical way:

> "Rod, how could we have a roof over our heads in our village, knowing the village next to us isn't so lucky? How could we walk with our roofing tin past other villages getting nothing? Just do your best and let us see."

How would NAFA respond to this request? On 5 May, ten days after the earthquake, the NAFA management committee met to decide its initial response to the earthquake. Committee meetings are open to all members, and some new members were attending their first meeting, motivated by the earthquake and the desire to help in some way. The meeting was extremely tense and emotions were running strong. Some members wanted to allocate all funds raised to the request received, knowing villagers were in desperate need in the immediate aftermath of the earthquake.

Others stressed NAFA's development mandate, and argued that we should leave the initial response to the Nepal government and international-aid agencies, whose mandate included disaster relief. These members argued we should save most of the NAFA-raised funds for the costly rebuilding stage to follow, pointing out that once dramatic media reporting of the earthquake damage faded, raising money to rebuild community infrastructure would be even more challenging.

However, nearly everyone, Nepalese-born and non-Nepalese committee members alike, indicated that they were not confident the Nepal government would respond adequately and in a timely manner to support earthquake victims. The government did not have a good track record of serving the needs of rural and remote communities and had a reputation for corruption and favouritism towards its own party officials and supporters. Many committee members also thought that the large, international disaster-relief agencies would primarily distribute aid in their trucks to the larger towns and rural villages accessible via the limited network of bitumen roads in Nepal.

Those who wanted NAFA to delay its response until the rebuild stage questioned how we could arrange the manufacture of roofing tin at a time when the demand would be great, and how it would be transported on roads damaged by the earthquake. Furthermore, we had heard that trucks were being commandeered by the government for the aid effort.

A further consideration was the need to find out how villages NAFA supported in the eastern districts of Solu Khumbu, Okhaldhunga and Dolakha had fared. Early indications were that they had not been significantly affected by the Gorkha earthquake. But a month later, on 12 May, a second large earthquake struck, its epicentre in the Everest area. At the meeting on 5 May, it had been assumed that the four NAFA-supported villages in eastern districts might need some help and that NAFA needed to hold back some funds for them.

At one point in the meeting, a NAFA member contended that village people were stoic enough to survive the monsoon with whatever they had salvaged, along with the aid they would probably receive from the Red Cross and other large agencies. Deb responded that while villagers were indeed stoic, the monsoon season was known for bringing additional health problems such as diarrhoeal and respiratory diseases. Being exposed to the wind, rain and humidity through lack of appropriate shelter, combined with inadequate food intake, could weaken already traumatised people and increase the incidence of respiratory and other monsoon-related illnesses.

Finally, after lengthy and sometimes heated argument, a memorable statement from someone attending their first NAFA committee meeting interrupted the discussion:

> "You are all living in an ivory tower. You can go home to your beds tonight, but right now villagers have nowhere to sleep. They need our help and they need it now!"

This stark reminder of the reality in the villages offended at least one committee member, who took the comment personally, later privately admonishing me for not bringing the new member 'into line'.

It was time for me to direct the discussion towards a conclusion. The views expressed ranged widely, from "do nothing right now" to "allocate as much as possible" of the funds raised in the pending earthquake appeal, perhaps topped up with funds from existing NAFA savings. A compromise approach was to "do something significant as an initial response", while holding back funds for needs that might arise in the eastern-district villages NAFA supported and for the rebuild stage that lay ahead.

NAFA had received a direct and clear request from a group of desperate villagers close to the epicentre of the Gorkha earthquake. Those villagers, who had been consulted by the HRDC, had identified immediate shelter and food as their most urgent priorities. Many people who had already made donations to the earthquake appeal expected those funds to be part of an initial NAFA response, to be transferred to Nepal as soon as possible to help earthquake victims survive the onset of the monsoon season.

I put forward a motion to allocate a moderate but substantial sum towards NAFA's initial response. The amount would comprise funds raised by the Nepalese community in Brisbane via the Nepalese Association of Queensland (NAQ) and funds raised by NAFA in the first week of its earthquake appeal. The initial allocation recognised the efforts of the Nepalese community to respond to the villagers' immediate needs through NAFA and for donor agencies to partner together where possible in responding to the earthquake.

At the time, I knew that much more would be needed to cover the cost of the request from the HRDC. We did not know how much would be needed for the rebuild response, but we knew it would be an exceedingly high figure for a totally volunteer-run organisation like NAFA. Still, it was time to act on the information we had and according to our capacity to respond to the initial crisis. The motion was passed unanimously.

Looking back on the meeting years later, we wonder if the division that occurred could have been managed better. The room was too small for the number of people attending, meaning not everyone was able to face others directly or hear clearly all that was said. I had tried to reassure everyone that not all funds raised would be spent on the initial response. However, that fear still existed for at least a few of the members present.

At the end of what was an exhausting meeting, several members, both regular attendees and those attending their first NAFA meeting, privately thanked me for facilitating such a difficult meeting and pledged their fundraising support. Although the consensus was that the right decision had been made, not everyone was happy. It could be argued, of course, that disagreement is normal and unavoidable during times of high stress and that tolerance is needed for personal expressions of frustration and compassion.

Four of the new attendees were to play important fundraising roles in the responses to follow. NAFA would soon make, for our size, very bold commitments to rebuild eight remote village schools and other community infrastructure, including the health post at Tawal. When finally estimated, the rebuilding costs, using earthquake-resistant construction techniques, would be more than 560 lakhs (AUD$700,000). Initially, it seemed an impossible target for a group used to raising AUD$40,000 to $50,000 per annum for development projects in Nepal.

NAFA had no funds to publicly advertise its earthquake appeal, nor were we on the Australian media's official list of organisations for public donations following the earthquake. But for now, our initial challenges were raising funds for roofing tin and rice, having the roofing tin manufactured, and then transporting the roofing tin and rice up to villages before the monsoon rains began in June, only a month away.

Chapter 11

Better you talk to them

For the next twelve days, I coordinated a campaign to raise the estimated AUD$175,000 needed to purchase rice and roofing tin. Those involved in the campaign were NAFA, the Nepalese Association of Queensland (NAQ), and other funding partners, including Smile Back to Me, Nepaleducaid, Namaste Enfant d'Himalayan in France, the British School of Kuwait and clients of Chandra's trekking agency, NEAT. We had less than a month to raise the funds.

In the villages, suffering continued as people cobbled together shelters with whatever they could salvage, mainly pieces of wood, torn bamboo matting and plastic-sheet roofing. These makeshift shelters would be wholly inadequate protection once the monsoon season brought high winds and at times torrential rain. During one particularly bad night, when Kanchha was meeting with local village leaders in the nearby village of Latab, a gust of high wind blew the plastic off the roof of his family's temporary shelter in Tawal. Terrified, his wife Lala sent Kanchha a message to hurry home.

While funds were being raised, a second significant earthquake struck Nepal, this time 7.3 in magnitude with its epicentre in the Solu Khumbu district, not far from Mount Everest. NAFA had provided funds to construct classrooms in four villages in the lower Solu Khumbu, Dolakha and Okhaldhunga districts. We now had a second remote area that needed support to rebuild education infrastructure.

On 18 May, a contract was signed with Hulas Steel Industries in Kathmandu to manufacture the corrugated-iron roofing sheets, and a week later, the rice was ordered. Both orders were made before there were sufficient funds to cover their cost, but with the monsoon rains fast approaching, time was of the essence. In addition to the challenge of raising the funds needed for the initial response, manufacturing and transport challenges lay ahead. I decided to fly to Kathmandu to help Chandra deal with suppliers and the transport issues face-to-face. I took with me some medical supplies donated by Wesley Hospital in Brisbane.

I arrived at the Kathmandu International Airport on 28 May, noticing the presence of the UN's World Food Program (WFP). After arriving at Chandra's home, over a cup of tea, Chandra said:

> "Rod, we have a problem".

Chandra had been in contact with 4WD-truck owners, who indicated they would be able to transport only two to three tons of roofing tin and rice per truckload from the end of the bitumen road in Dhading Bensi up to the Tawal area, at a cost of 23,000 Nrs (AUD$288) per truckload. With an estimated 150 tons to transport, this added between AUD$14,000 and $20,000 to the budget, funds NAFA did not have.

It would also be exceptionally difficult to organise the deliveries, as trucks were being quarantined by the government for earthquake relief. In addition, the treacherous five-hour 4WD track to the end of the road head near Tawal had been severely damaged by the earthquake. Even if the roads were not already impassable, it would be virtually impossible to transport all the roofing sheets and rice before monsoon rains closed the road.

Chandra contacted a friend who owned a helicopter, but was told this option would be extremely expensive. Instead, he suggested Chandra contact the UN's WFP, based at the airport, which was providing free helicopter transport of relief goods. We decided to give it a go. Chandra looked up the WFP Logistics Cluster number on the UN website and dialled, handing the phone to me.

"They will be foreigners, Rod. Better you talk to them."

As I took the phone from Chandra, I thought:

> "Why would they help? Surely, they would be too busy to talk to us, such a small player in the overall relief effort."

I was connected to the section responsible for coordinating support, including road and helicopter transport of goods. Much to our surprise and relief, the head of the area was encouraging, offering to meet with us next day.

> "Before then, you need to download the online transport-assistance request form, complete it, and bring it in with you tomorrow."

Chandra and I made several visits to the WFP Logistics Cluster office at the airport between 29 May and 2 June. During these visits, we were told that the Russian-built helicopter used to transport relief goods to earthquake-affected areas was too big to land on the schoolgrounds in Tawal. An alternative landing site, 50 metres by 50 metres, needed to be identified. Guided by Chandra's knowledge of the area, the WFP staff member surveyed the area using Google Earth. We agreed on a site at Latab (coordinates recorded at the time N28.05'17.43 E84.59'09.56). Three terraces would need to be cleared of a maize crop and flattened to prepare the landing site required. The 'can do' villagers sheltering in Latab laboured for twenty-four hours to prepare the landing zone. Farmers were compensated for losing their crop and having to clear out the stone-wall terrace boundaries.

It was a trying time for everyone, including Chandra and his family. On the day of the earthquake, family members had crawled on hands and knees away from their house, the earth shaking beneath them. Five weeks after the earthquake, they were still sleeping in tents in their driveway, too frightened to stay overnight in their home. They were, of course, also worried about villagers in the Tawal area, and others affected by the earthquakes and aftershocks.

I said I would be fine to sleep in an upstairs bedroom in Chandra's house, having not experienced the trauma of the earthquake. It was hot and humid, so I went to bed wearing not much at all. On my second night in Kathmandu, having just fallen asleep, I was awoken by the loud bang of an aftershock. My heart began to thump as I awoke with a start, scrambling to put on shorts and glasses. I could hear Chandra outside shouting:

> "Rod, get out of the house".

After what was probably two minutes, I made it down the stairs and out of the house, joining the others in tents that night. The next morning Chandra scolded me:

> "Rod, if you plan to sleep in the house, you need to be able to get out of it in 20 seconds".

> "Yes, I will, Chandra. Sorry," I replied sheepishly.

However, unable to resist a comfortable mattress, I again slept in the house the following night. When I joined Chandra and his family for breakfast next morning, he asked how I had slept.

> "Not that great, Chandra. I was ready to get out of the house in 20 seconds, but I have to tell you, it isn't easy sleeping with your glasses on!"

After a short hesitation, Chandra and his wife burst out laughing. A shared joke was a welcome release in the high-stress situation.

That same day, I received welcome news from the President of the NAQ. An additional allocation was going to be made towards NAFA's initial response. That meant the total amount raised would be enough to cover the cost of the roofing sheets and rice ordered. The response from the public had been humbling. NAFA, NAQ and small volunteer-run NGOs in Spain, France and Austria had drawn on the goodwill of their networks to raise not only the funds required to provide roofing tin and rice for every family in the VDC, but also enough for NAFA's other initial response commitments in eastern Nepal and Thimi in the Kathmandu Valley. I was ecstatic and relieved.

Negotiations with WFP staff continued, at times appearing chaotic. At first, they wanted to wait until all the rice (already in Dhading Bensi) and roofing tin (at the time still being manufactured) was in Dhading Bensi before they would start the airlift. But there was a hiccup with the roofing sheets. After much negotiation, the Hulas agent agreed on a 4 June delivery date to the end of the bitumen road in the district capital, Dhading Bensi. On that day, the roofing sheets arrived, but were not colour-bonded. Hulas acknowledged they had made an error in the paperwork and agreed to re-do the order, selling the roofing sheets that had arrived in the local hardware store.

After many meetings with the roofing-tin agent, we negotiated an 11 June delivery date. We separated the rice and roofing-tin applications for transport assistance, and WFP Logistics Cluster staff agreed to move the first helicopter-load of rice the next day. Chandra, his nephew Yuddha, myself, and Avinash Singh, a representative from the NAQ visiting family in Kathmandu at the time, boarded the WFP-hired helicopter in Kathmandu, flying to Dhading Bensi to pick up the first load of rice.

In Dhading Bensi, more than ten volunteers from the Tawal area greeted us at the landing zone, ready to load the rice. It was an exceedingly difficult time for these young men. They were living in tents in Dhading Bensi and providing 24-hour security for the rice and roofing sheets. It was a lot to ask at a time when their families were in shock and surviving perilous living conditions back in their villages.

The original landing zone in Dhading Bensi was too dusty for the helicopter and had to be moved closer to the river, but with monsoon rains now coming regularly, steadily rising river levels threatened the condition of the rice and roofing sheets, as well as the safety of the men guarding the precious cargo. Tarpaulin sheeting was the only protection. As the move dragged on and the challenges increased, we agreed to pay the men a modest amount in recognition of their efforts under very trying conditions.

The Latab landing zone also presented logistical challenges. Before any helicopter could land, the helipad had to be hand-watered for two hours to minimise the dust. A roster was set up: each village would take turns coming to Latab in the early morning, where villagers would prepare the helipad for landing, then organise logistics, checking off each name on the register as the rice and roofing sheets were distributed. They would then return to their village at the end of the day with their rice or roofing-sheet allocation.

Local leaders greeted us in Latab with 'khatas' (greeting scarves) as we arrived with the first helicopter cargo of rice. A regular visitor, I was a familiar face to them, relieved to be arriving with much-needed rice. I have been back to the landing zone many times since and feel quite emotional each time. But on that day, it was serious business – I just wanted the helicopter unloaded and the rice distributed. An underlying feeling of sadness would be delayed until the next day when I hiked down to Tawal and visited the school.

As the distribution of rice got underway over subsequent days, I addressed leaders and local families. I expressed sadness on behalf of all donors, and confirmed that NAFA and its funding partners would stand by them during their time of greatest need. I also expressed confidence that local villagers would draw on their extraordinary strength, skills and resilience to rebuild their communities, with outside donor help, in the months and years to follow.

Avinash, Yuddha and I stayed in a US Aid-donated tent at the school in Latab. Locals said Latab was the only village in the area safe from landslide risk. The only structure standing in the village was the small, concrete toilet block at the school, built by the Kadoorie Welfare Association (Gurkhas). Chandra returned in the helicopter to continue coordinating the uplifts from Kathmandu.

Over the next few days, I experienced a taste of the intermittent distribution pattern that would prove to be the norm during the month-long helicopter uplift. No helicopters arrived on 6 June, which was a public holiday for the pilots! Then, after some loads arrived on 7 June, we were told that once again that no helicopters would be arriving the following day, as the helicopter was due for its monthly maintenance check. We were disappointed and frustrated, but understood that patience was needed. At least we were on the schedule for relief-aid deliveries, for which we were extremely grateful.

Late on the morning of 8 June, we heard a helicopter approaching from the valley below. A small Buddhist welfare organisation had been told about the Latab helipad and decided to arrive unannounced with some donated goods. The sudden arrival reflected the lack of coordination in the earthquake-relief effort, with many well-intentioned groups simply turning up unannounced. The problem was that the helipad had not been watered!

I ran with the other villagers towards the helipad, fearing what would happen when the helicopter landed. As expected, a large cloud of dust billowed into the air, obscuring the helicopter. By the time I arrived, the pilot had somehow managed to land. The door opened and staff jumped out to unload the goods. The outraged Russian pilot appeared at the door when the unloading was completed and thundered in English:

> "Everyone back into the helicopter. We won't be coming back, as it is too dangerous."

I shouted back, the engine still running:

> "You need to give us warning that you are coming so we can water the helipad".

The pilot scowled and took off in another tsunami of dust. I knew word would get back quickly to WFP Logistical Cluster staff. Was this the end of the uplift? Would pilots refuse to land in Latab for safety reasons? I immediately called our WFP contact and explained what had happened.

> "Ok, we are sorry for that. We will forewarn you in the future when any helicopters are being sent", he replied.

A potential disaster had been averted. In fact, the Russian pilot came back many times and quickly warmed to the villagers. It helped that they fed him 'daal bhat', Nepal's staple meal of lentils, rice and vegetables, while he waited for his helicopter to be unloaded. Where the Nepalese pilots flew more cautiously, with 1.8 to two-ton loads, he usually came loaded to the helicopter's registered capacity of 2.5 tons!

I stayed in Latab for four days, assessing earthquake damage, talking to local leaders and witnessing the start of the rice distribution to villagers. Kanchha took me down through the villages of Dhuseni, Tawal and Tawal Bensi. Devastation was everywhere. I took a photo of Kanchha and the main builder in the area, Buddha Tamang, to show the wreckage to NAFA supporters back home. Buddha had built much of the infrastructure in the area funded by NAFA and others. Looking sadly at the destruction, he asked in a soft voice:

> "How could this happen? I thought I was a good builder."

We stopped at the school in Tawal that NAFA, Smile Back to Me and Nepaleducaid had rebuilt and extended to Grade 10. The school lay in ruins, with only the timber roof trusses and roofing sheets left largely intact. Kanchha and I sat quietly amidst the rubble, heads down and deep in thought. Kanchha broke the silence.

> "We feel so sorry, Rod. You and NAFA supporters have worked so hard to find the money to build this school and now look at it!"

I replied, fighting back tears:

> "Please don't worry Kanchha. You have enough responsibility on your shoulders. Back home, we are not affected like your community is, and we will help you rebuild this school."

Years later we can talk about this moment when we both felt overwhelmed by what lay ahead but knew we had the close personal and community bonds that would see us through.

The health post and its furniture were also damaged beyond repair. The medicine cabinet lay on its side, where Lila Maya had emptied its contents in the aftermath of the earthquake.

Kanchha and I made our way down to the power station near Tawal Bensi, passing another group of families who had set themselves up in temporary shelters. The power-station walls were all cracked, and the instrument panels ruined, but the generator and turbine looked intact.

On the way back through Dhuseni, we were told that a medical team from Pokhara had arrived, again unannounced, to provide medical care for earthquake victims. But by now, six weeks after the earthquake, the injured had all been treated or evacuated to hospital. So, with good intentions, the doctors and nurses in the camp were giving advice on general hygiene, hand-washing and tooth-brushing. The local Tawal health-post Coordinator, Beg, said that while the medical support since the earthquake had been appreciated, he wished they had contacted him when they arrived.

> "Sometimes, the doctors distribute medicine that required repeats that I don't have here in the health post. Following these visits, villagers often come to me, not knowing what the medicine given to them was for. It would be better if we could coordinate our treatment to earthquake victims."

One of the members of the Pokhara medical team asked us where we were staying while in the area. When I replied that I was staying in Latab, the team member commented:

> "We had planned to go up there tomorrow, but because of the landslide risks between Dhuseni and Latab, we have decided not to go".

On the trek back up to Latab, Kanchha and I approached the area where rocks had continued to sporadically tumble down from the hills above. At the time, villagers in Serchet and Dhuseni feared a large landslide. Kanchha could see villagers higher on the track coming down from Latab. "Is it safe to go?" we asked. After receiving a hopeful, "We think so", we scampered across the rubble of rocks that covered that section of the track and continued the steep ascent to Latab.

On the third day of the uplift, I joined villagers on a large boulder where they sat, waiting for the helicopter to arrive from Dhading Bensi. I was standing as the helicopter approached from the valley below. The tiny hand of a child tugged on my pant leg, motioning me to sit. I did so and seconds later, the downdraft from the helicopter nearly pushed us both over as it flew past to land. I realised that had I stayed on my feet, I would probably have ended up broken and battered at the bottom of the steep slope!

On 15 June, ten days after the first airlift, the distribution of rice to 1,225 families in twenty-five villages was completed. Two days later, the uplift of roofing sheets commenced. Monsoon rains were now a regular occurrence, so each day, WFP Logistic Cluster staff and the pilot would decide whether there would be any helicopter trips that day. Back in Brisbane, it was a never-ending emotional roller-coaster ride as we woke early each morning racked with anxiety as we checked our computer for news from the previous day. There were tears of disappointment and frustration on days when no uplifts were possible.

It was an incredibly stressful time, knowing villagers were in makeshift shelters, waiting anxiously for their allocation of roofing sheets. Sometimes, they arrived in Latab for their allocation, only to be prevented from returning home by the monsoon rains. On one such occasion, 150 aid recipients from another village were stuck in Latab after big storms hit the area.

Finally, on 8 July, a month after the uplift began, the roof-sheeting distribution was complete. NAFA, its funding partners and the local villagers who benefited from the life-saving supplies will be forever grateful for WFP assistance when it was most needed.

The WFP, through a local aid agency, Himalayan Health Care, would later implement another very practical initiative. Himalayan Health Care would allocate 150 kg of rice and 27 kg of 'daal' to each family in return for twenty days' community recovery work, such as repairing paths and preparing a local helipad for future emergency evacuations.

With the most immediate food and shelter needs addressed, NAFA now had to raise funds to rebuild remote community infrastructure, including four schools, a health post and agricultural cooperative infrastructure in the Tawal area, a further four schools in eastern Nepal and more.

NAFA's rebuilding response to the earthquakes would be a real test for its community development approach, both in Nepal and in Australia. The context had just become much more complex. We would need to understand earthquake-resistant building standards and become more engaged with the government bureaucracy in Nepal. We would also need to work with architects and engineers, both in Australia and in Nepal. And, most importantly, we would need to identify new funding sources to finance the rebuild program.

NAFA's urgent community infrastructure rebuild commitments again seemed overwhelming. We had to trust that affected communities would have the capacity, strength and problem-solving ability to manage all the responsibilities associated with the rebuild program. But first, we needed to make sure that infrastructure would be rebuilt in areas safe from landslide risk and in accordance with earthquake-resistant building codes.

Chapter 12

What you are feeling is what we are feeling

The distribution of roofing sheets and rice was complete. Villagers managed to plant some crops and braced themselves for the monsoon season. Their long-term continued existence in the area was threatened. Significant challenges would have to be overcome before villagers could rebuild their homes and community infrastructure.

Apart from the difficulties of raising the funds needed to rebuild, the Nepal government had announced that rebuilding could occur only after an area had been declared safe from landslide risk. This pronouncement included a commitment by the government to send teams of geotechnical engineers to affected areas, where they would undertake landslide assessments and prepare reports on their findings.

Once an area had been declared safe from landslide risk, government approval of school site plans and classroom design was required before rebuilding could finally begin. Classrooms had to be built using earthquake-resistant techniques, meaning local builders would need specialised training. All these considerations more than doubled the cost per classroom of previous classroom constructions, which meant a lot more fundraising.

In July 2015, NAQ invited us to an earthquake response workshop in Brisbane they had organised. In attendance were several Nepal-born engineers. They had migrated to Australia many years before and were now working in various positions in state government departments, universities and the private sector. Also present were two young Brisbane-based architects, Rara K.C. and Marie Penny, who approached me during a coffee break.

> "We would like to help in some way. Perhaps we could write a simple, practical guide that would be useful for local builders in the villages NAFA will be supporting in the rebuild program?"

We appreciated their enthusiasm and especially their willingness to do something practical.

Within three months, Rara and Marie had prepared *A Guidebook for Earthquake-Resistant Non-Engineered Stone Construction,* a practical text to help local villagers rebuild their houses and community infrastructure using earthquake-resistant design and construction techniques. The *Guidebook* was written in plain English, with many diagrams and pictures to illustrate key building concepts, including: creating good foundations, building a 'box', using steel rods, installing tie beams and bands, constructing buttresses, locating doors and windows, and installing metal plates for roof trusses.

Useful feedback on early drafts of the *Guidebook* was provided by engineers in Brisbane's Nepalese community, including Narayan Pokharel. This was the beginning of a series of connections between professionals in Brisbane and Nepal that played a critical role in the ultimate success of the rebuild program. Again, the importance of fostering strong relationships with those who could either help directly or knew someone who could was critical.

Kathmandu-based architect Sabin Shrestha, a former colleague of Rara's, developed a 3D visual and accompanying one-page Nepali-language summary of earthquake-resistant construction. This summary and the *Guidebook* were taken to local builders in villages NAFA had made a commitment to support in the rebuilding phase. They were great tools for exposing builders to the basic concepts of earthquake-resistant building techniques. A few builders were found to have previous experience with these techniques, having worked with them on projects outside the local area.

Sabin also kindly agreed to prepare the site plans and classroom/health post designs NAFA would need for the rebuild program. In October and November 2015, we returned to Nepal, visiting the Tawal area twice. It was Deb's first visit since the earthquake. We were greeted at the entrance to the schoolgrounds by local leaders and a small group of subdued villagers. This was not the time for the usual exuberant welcome program. Although she had seen photos of the destruction, Deb was not prepared for the reality she confronted. She surveyed the wreckage of the school briefly before bursting into tears, triggering a similar reaction in me. For a moment no-one looked up or spoke. Then three women came to Deb and gently wrapped their arms around her.

> "'I am sorry. It's just so sad', Deb said tearfully.
>
> 'That's ok, Deborah Aunty. What you are feeling is what we are feeling.'"

School lessons were being conducted throughout the VDC, utilising temporary classrooms such as tents, steel-pole structures with roofing sheets or, in a few cases, the ruins of earthquake-damaged classrooms.

Local leaders organised a meeting, attended by sixty villagers from five villages in the area. They indicated that apart from the initial emergency helicopter landings by the Nepal Army to evacuate the most seriously injured earthquake victims, no-one from the government had visited the area in the seven months since. They identified a geotechnical assessment of landslide risk as their most urgent need. Those attending expressed appreciation that we had already made an appointment to meet with the Chief District Officer in Dhading Bensi on our return journey to Kathmandu. I also confirmed that NAFA would help rebuild four of the schools in the area: Tawal, Latab, Kutal and Richet. Local builders at the meeting acknowledged the need for training in earthquake-resistant construction, though at least three local builders had some outside experience with using iron rods and concrete pillars.

At the meeting, Deb circulated two photo books she had produced as part of her oral-history project. One was a pictorial history of Tawal village. Deb's introduction read:

> "The earthquake took lives and destroyed all the housing and community structures. I hope this picture history will help keep alive the memories of a beautiful village and the courageous people who live there."

The other was a photo book of everyday life as it had been prior to the destruction caused by the Gorkha earthquake. In its introduction, Deb wrote:

> "The buildings are lost but the spirit and skills of the people endure. Tawal will rise again and people will continue to work hard and enjoy their lives. Those who died in the earthquake will not be forgotten. There is hope for a better future."

Everyone gathered around to go through the photo books, smiling as they did so. The books provided at least temporary respite from the uncertain future they faced.

For seven months, local villagers had been waiting for geotechnical experts to come up to the area to assess the risks of future landslides. The government had promised to undertake such assessments, but this had not occurred in most areas, including the Ree VDC. On our return trip to Kathmandu, Kanchha and two other HRDC representatives joined me for a meeting with the Chief District Officer in Dhading Bensi to discuss the delay. When I asked the Chief District Officer if they were planning to undertake a geotechnical assessment of the Ree VDC soon, he replied that the government was currently focussed on the new constitution, so he was not sure if and when they would do any more assessments.

I asked whether, if NAFA was able to organise a geotechnical assessment, the district office would recognise its findings. He replied stiffly that he was waiting for new 'Rules and Regulations' that would give him the authority to approve such assessments. His final throw-away comment, said with a hint of a smile and in a condescending tone, is still vivid in my memory.

> "Well, if people are still living in the area, then they must think it is safe from landslides. Why else would they stay there?"

I glanced over at community members, who were looking down at the floor, devastated and shaking their heads. They knew they would have to go it alone, as they always had in the past. It was obvious that the district head office cared little about what happened in the hilly areas some distance from district headquarters. It was a reflection of the deep-seated feudal mindset and caste discrimination that continues to exist in Nepal.

On the second visit in November, Kalpana Kaphle, a Nepal-born, Brisbane social worker, joined us, having also been inspired by the earthquake response workshop in July. She took annual leave to come to Nepal and facilitate some post-trauma recovery activities in a school in Thimi, supported by NAFA, and then in Tawal.

Kalpana and Deb, supported by local women Yuna Tamang and Sabita Tamang, met with 100 women to identify their immediate needs and priorities. Not surprisingly, they said they were still experiencing major psychological issues such as grief and loss of 'what was'. Fear and anxiety remained, as they were unsure whether it was safe to rebuild their homes and community infrastructure. The ongoing stress from the trauma was also causing other health complaints, including gynaecological problems.

In addition to the commitments NAFA and its donor partners had made to rebuild their school and health post, local women identified the repair of water infrastructure, the micro-hydro system and their agricultural cooperative infrastructure as their main priorities. They also identified as important some form of skills training that would allow them to earn an income and rebuild their livelihoods in the aftermath of the earthquake.

Over the next few days in Tawal, Kalpana and Deb, with help from teachers, facilitated trauma-recovery activities with a total of 343 students in Nursery, Grade 1 and Grades 6 to 10. As the activities were occurring seven months after the earthquake, the concept and consequences of trauma were addressed indirectly. The workshops were designed to be fun, building resilience and coping skills, while at the same time preventing any trauma-related mental-health issues from escalating.

Students were encouraged to identify significant incidents and associated feelings of sadness and happiness, as well as how feelings can affect the body. They discussed strategies on how to manage strong feelings in a positive rather than a harmful way. The overall aim of the activities was for students to gain a sense of personal power and control, feeling safe and protected within their community. Students and teachers expressed appreciation to Kalpana for her professionalism, empathy and enthusiasm in taking time off from her work and coming to the village to offer help to students still feeling fear and uncertainty.

When we returned to Kathmandu, Chandra and I met with two geotechnical engineers referred by Nepali engineers in Brisbane. On 3 December, one of those engineers, Professor Megh Dhital from Tribhuvan University, travelled, by jeep then on foot, to Tawal to undertake a four-day 'rapid assessment' of villages in the Ree VDC. Villagers were so grateful Professor Dhital had taken the time to come up to do the assessment that Kanchha wrote on Facebook:

> "Today all villagers of Tawal and Kutal got so much happy because Professor Dhital has arrived from Kathmandu to check all land of Ree VDC".

Given the short time available, we originally asked that he prioritise those villages NAFA and its funding partners had committed to help with the rebuild of community infrastructure. However, Professor Dhital recognised the villagers' vulnerable situation and worked from dawn until dusk to visit every village in the Ree VDC, including Kichet, 1,000 metres above Tawal and the village most impacted by the earthquake.

NAFA received a detailed report from Professor Dhital within a month. Professor Dhital advised that, except for Kichet, it would be safe for villagers to rebuild their houses and schools. However, two gabion walls would need to be built above the school at Tawal and above Tawal village. He also advised that the Tawal health post could not be rebuilt in the same location, due to the risk of landslide from the hills above. The task of securing a new site for the health post would prove challenging. We will return to that challenge in Chapter 14.

Sabin, Kalpana, Professor Dhital, engineers from the Nepalese community in Brisbane, together with others in Nepal, were all competent, compassionate Nepali professionals, whose contributions to the initial earthquake response were invaluable. Other contributions would follow to support the rebuilding program.

Professor Dhital's report provided villagers with the confidence they needed to feel safe about staying in the area. His rapid assessment of landslide risk represented an important earthquake recovery milestone. It was time to start rebuilding community infrastructure and the livelihoods of local villagers.

Chandra's parents, Kaishya and Daman Dup Tamang, greet us on our first visit to Tawal in 2006

Elders chant *Maane Dori*, naming the monasteries/ villages visited on their journey 300+ years ago from Tibet to Tawal

Inside dark, damp classrooms in 2006

Early HRDC meeting

First NAFA-sponsored science teacher – Dipak Pandey

Raul Accion and Rod with three of the Grade 10 students from Tawal school sponsored by NAFA and SBTM for further education, Nisha, Gobinda and Kumar

Tawal school 2013 (pre-earthquake) with health post on terrace above the school

NAFA-sponsored health workers, Sunita, Lila Maya and Beg, in front of the original health post

Beg testing blood with microscope

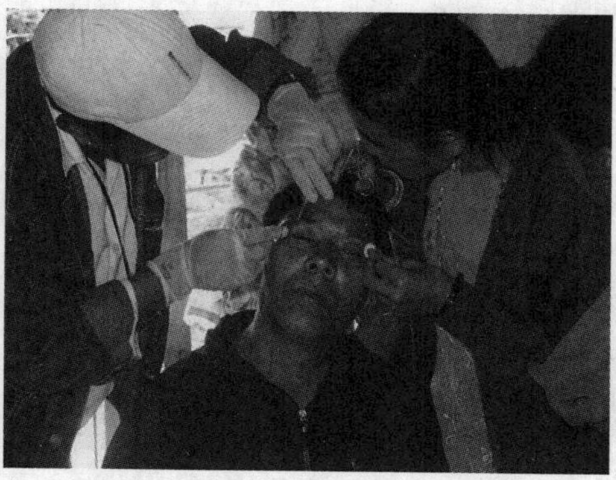

Beg and Lila Maya stitching a local villager's wound

NAFA-sponsored Ashok (middle) assembles turbine at micro-hydro station

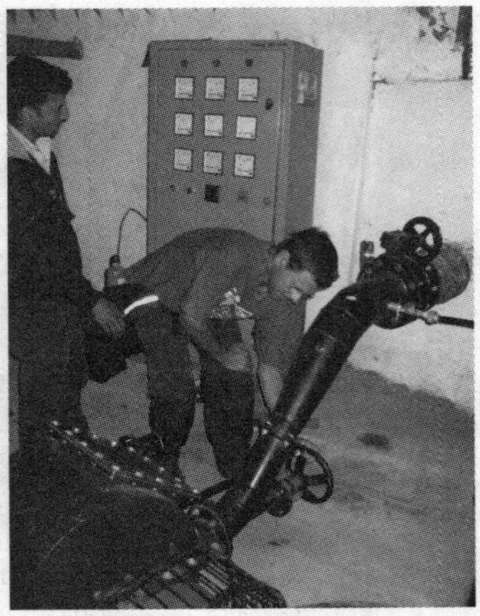

Rod opens valve to turn on electricity

Jus Bahadur gains access to electricity and makes furniture for whole VDC, comprising 25 villages

Students and teacher (Ramesh) gain access to 10 new computers at school

Elderly villager using traditional cooking stove

Damador Karki with villager and her improved cooking stove

Brishya rummages through remains of what was her house in Dhuseni

Mika with her mother Kanchhi Maya in Dhading Bensi field hospital

Kanchha and Buddha, still in shock viewing earthquake destruction

Kanchha looks so sad in what was a classroom at the school in Tawal

Health post after the 2015 earthquake

Inside micro-hydro power station

Tara teaching Class 3 in temporary classroom

Classes held in earthquake-damaged classroom

Loading rice onto WFP helicopter at Dhading Bensi

Villagers return home with 60 kg of rice

And 12 sheets of roofing tin

Unannounced helicopter arrives at Latab but the helipad had not been watered!

Government-accredited Khora Tamang provides earthquake-resistant building training

Kanchha Dong, Sirap, Buddha and Suk Lama proudly displaying training certificates

Villager breaking down stone through a thong to make aggregate

Local stonemason chisels out a stone brick

Passing the trays of concrete laying slab for two-storey classroom at Tawal

Appreciative students in new classroom at Richet

Deborah hands over the keys to Lok, Principal of rebuilt school at Latab

Rod hands over the keys to new fifteen-classroom hub school at Tawal to Deepak, President of the School Management Committee

A very happy Kanchha!

Tirha Maya leads dance at opening ceremony

Mendho Maya dance ends opening ceremony

Students brush teeth after tiffin

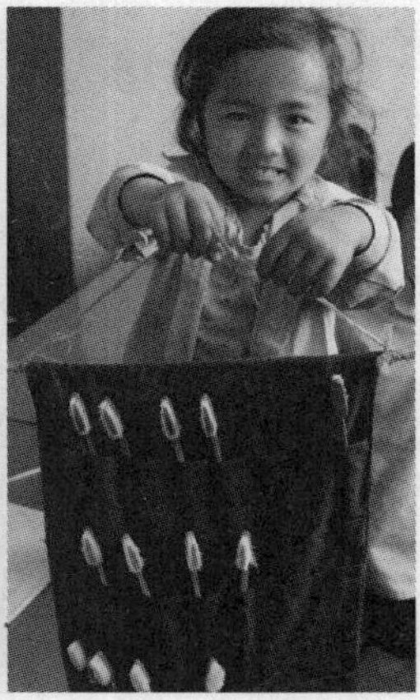

Arpana enthusiastically holds toothbrush holder

Health workers set up temporary health posts after earthquake in damaged church: Beg, Sunita and Lila Maya

Happy and healthy Manju and Malika: "Beg saved our lives during childbirth"

Handover of 'Jamunapari' goat to Ram Maya

Ram Kumari, Soinam and other women attending early morning adult literacy classes

Swikriti sewing tote bags

Deb and Rebika with tailors looking at material for tote bags

Rasmita and Pema proudly displaying their tote bags

Cooperative members in front of high-tech nursery

Sagar (caretaker) watering plants inside nursery

Kanchha and Ramesh with
donated computer

Man Bahadur B.K. (Dalit metalworker) with arm through goat carcass to heat metal

Meeting with members of Dalit community

Chapter 13

Not within our lifetime

Professor Dhital had given the go-ahead to rebuild community infrastructure, except for the health post at Tawal, which could not be rebuilt on the same site due to landslide risk. However, many challenges lay ahead, including government bureaucracy, funding, technical design, local builders' capacity to rebuild the infrastructure to earthquake-resistant standards, the high cost of transport, and building seasons limited by annual monsoon rains.

NAFA and its like-minded partners faced the daunting challenge of collectively raising over AUD$700,000 from our respective donor networks. Our supporters had already given generously to fund an initial response to the earthquake and we now needed them to provide even greater financial support to the rebuild phase, while continuing their loyal support to nine ongoing NAFA education, health and childcare programs. Then there were the logistics of coordinating the rebuild of community infrastructure across eight villages (four in the Tawal area and four in eastern Nepal) with a limited number of skilled tradesmen in each village. These builders also faced family pressure to prioritise rebuilding their own homes and those of relatives.

Drawing on our community development framework, we needed to negotiate agreements on site plans and classroom designs with the community and the government. We had to maximise community participation in the rebuild, including their volunteer contribution, to help make funds raised in our earthquake appeal go further. We needed to strengthen and then trust the capacity of the local community to implement the rebuilding phase. Finally, we had to monitor implementation, to ensure that expenditure remained within budget and construction was in accordance with earthquake-resistant standards.

The first challenge was the Nepalese bureaucracy. The government sought to coordinate the rebuild and avoid duplication by requiring international-aid agencies to register their offer to rebuild school classrooms in specified villages. A local NGO had to lodge a 'Request Letter' at the Department of Education (DoE) office in Sano Thimi, just outside Kathmandu. In the spirit of partnership and wanting to drive funds raised by NAFA further, I asked a departmental officer if the government would be interested in a 50–50 funding partnership with NAFA in rebuilding school classrooms.

> "'No, we want to find out which international-aid agencies have a relationship with local villages, and we will try and rebuild where that relationship doesn't exist,' was his response."

A Memorandum of Understanding (MOU) had to be prepared, using a template provided by the DoE. The MOU had to be co-signed before 15 December 2015 by a locally registered NGO and the Department. If not signed by that date, the registration process would have to start all over again, through the Social Welfare Council in Nepal rather than through the DoE. Fearful that process would be even more lengthy and bureaucratic than working through the DoE and the department responsible for building construction in Nepal, the Department of Urban Development and Building Construction (DUDBC), Chandra, Kanchha and I worked hard to meet the 15 December deadline for planned NAFA-supported school rebuilds in four villages in Ree VDC.

The MOU had to be accompanied by a Funding Agreement between the local NGO and its principle donor. School site plans for each school being rebuilt and architectural classroom designs were supposed to be approved by the DUDBC within thirty days of signing the MOU. School plans had to incorporate the government model number of classrooms: eight classrooms for schools going up to Grade 5, and fifteen classrooms for schools going up to Grade 10. Classroom plans also had to consider student class sizes. For NAFA, this meant lodging classroom plans that would cater for either twenty-four students or thirty-six students, the largest class size allowed.

After significant delays, the Nepal government released government pre-approved classroom designs incorporating steel trusses. If the local NGO did not use the government-provided classroom designs, which were publicised in guidelines many months after the earthquake, it had to have its alternative plans approved by a DUDBC engineer. If the proposed classroom design used wooden roof trusses, the plans had to be accompanied by a certificate signed by a structural engineer, at the donors' expense.

Other designs were brought to NAFA's attention by engineers and NAFA supporters in Australia, including mud-brick and all-steel designs. However, these suggestions did not take into consideration the context of the school rebuilding, including distance from steel manufacturers, road access and the soil type in the area.

None of the schools was in a village accessible by road. They were, however, in areas where good-quality stone was available, though those stones had to be shaped into 'bricks' by local stonemasons. Some stone 'bricks' from classrooms destroyed by the earthquake could be reused, at least for the first phase of the rebuild. The supply of stones would undoubtedly run out, due to the large quantity of stone needed to build the number of classrooms required under the new guidelines that supplemented the existing building code.

The new guidelines for class sizes meant that, in most cases, existing roof trusses would be too small for reuse. However, steel trusses would be very costly, particularly as they would need to be transported from the manufacturer to the end of the road head and then carried by men to the villages.

Sabin and local HRDC leaders agreed that stone construction should be used, with timber roof trusses and corrugated, galvanised-iron roofs. The preparation of architectural classroom designs proved particularly challenging, due to ever-changing government building codes, limitations in land size available in all four villages, and the number and size of classrooms required.

A structural engineer was contracted to provide the certificate required to accompany the technical designs for twenty-four and thirty-six student classrooms submitted for DoE approval. NAFA and Sabin worked with representatives from the Speedway Foundation and the HRDC to register an offer to help rebuild a total of forty-six classrooms in seven villages, including thirty-five classrooms in four Dhading district villages: Tawal, Kutal, Latab and Richet. Another eleven classrooms would be substantially rebuilt with NAFA funds in a school in eastern Nepal but did not have to be included in the MOU with the DoE.

The MOU was signed on the deadline, 15 December 2015. But it would be six months before final approvals from the DoE and DUDBC were obtained. A general building code existed in Nepal at the time, but a specific set of guidelines was developed and published online by the government after the earthquake. They also published brochures to support the guidelines.

Sabin prepared classroom-design drawings that were consistent with the building code. However, on a few occasions, measurements varied slightly from the guidelines and the designs were rejected by DUDBC engineers without any reasons given, meaning drawings had to be redone several times.

> "We experienced significant delays because DUDBC only had a few engineers. They were trying to be cooperative, but more engineers should have been appointed after the earthquake. Government offices are too slow in Nepal. I am sorry to say that, but it is true. We have had to get used to it when you work in Nepal."

I met with Sabin many times before his workday started. I often got lost in the maze of streets surrounding Durbar Square, depending on where Chandra had let me off on his way to work. I would look for one of the small cafes on Freak Street (Jhhonchen Tole), the name given to it by locals during the 1960s when hippies used to congregate in the street's popular hashish cafes. Sabin would arrive on his motorbike and after walking up several dimly lit stairs, find a spot to sit, and order hot lemon tea that soothed our dry throats on the cold Kathmandu mornings. His smiling, bespectacled (like me) face was always comforting as he calmly discussed and resolved many challenges we faced before and during the rebuild.

I subsequently asked Sabin how he felt about all the architectural support he provided NAFA after the earthquake at low cost, incorporating many hours of unpaid work.

> "I loved working with NAFA. It was a new experience. I had a chance to work precisely. I did the budget estimates and all the material quantities. Normally we just do the

> drawings and not detailed estimates. I had to make many changes because of the various site challenges and different-size classrooms needed. But I enjoyed the preciseness of the work with NAFA. I knew foreigners were helping with funding the rebuild of schools in my country and I wanted to make sure the estimates were as accurate as possible."

In the meantime, funds were still being raised towards the target of AUD$700,000, a figure that seemed totally out of reach. As a small, totally volunteer-run organisation, NAFA was used to raising between AUD$40,000 and $50,000 per annum in addition to donations earmarked for its ongoing programs. Supporters were being asked to continue their annual donations towards nine ongoing education, health and childcare programs and then to dig deep for NAFA's earthquake appeal.

Realistically, how long would fundraising take? We assumed up to five years, but in the villages, local builders thought much longer. Two of the three main builders in Tawal, Buddha and Sirap, went together to see the school not long after the earthquake struck and were shocked to see so much damage. They said they felt very emotional after they had put so much effort into building the classrooms.

> "Neither of us felt that the school would be rebuilt within our lifetime."

In Kutal, Dipak's father died in the earthquake, one of eighteen fatalities in that village. A few days after the earthquake, Dipak went up to the school and was devastated by what he saw. He thought:

> "Maybe we could rebuild with NAFA's help in 15 years if this earthquake has not also struck Australia."

There were also formidable local site challenges. In Tawal and Latab, additional land had to be sourced and purchased from adjoining private landowners. For Tawal, it meant that two-storey classroom blocks would need to be built in an area considered safe from landslide risk. For Latab, the additional land was needed to build eight classrooms, the number required by the Nepal government for schools going to Grade 5.

But before rebuilding could commence, local builders needed training in earthquake-resistant construction techniques. It took time to source engineers willing to go to remote areas to conduct week-long training programs. In February 2016, I went to Nepal to meet three prospective engineers, who quoted on conducting the training programs. Again, important contacts and help with preparing the briefs were provided by Nepal-born engineers now residing in Brisbane. After obtaining three quotes, NAFA signed a contract with the government-accredited Institute for Suitable Actions for Prosperity to undertake two seven-day earthquake-resistance training programs: in Tawal, for schools to be rebuilt in the Dhading district, and in Shyama, for schools to be rebuilt in eastern Nepal. Training by two engineers and a stonemason was conducted in November 2016, with a total of thirty-four builders from seven schools and school-construction committee overseers attending.

The earthquake-resistant building plans were complex and undoubtedly difficult to read for village builders. The three main builders in Tawal had never been to school, their parents having insisted they stay home and help look after their land. They were very competent and honest builders, but although one had taught himself to read and write, the plans were still going to be a challenge.

Ordering building materials would be similarly complex, especially as the HRDC planned to coordinate the purchase of building materials in bulk, then allocate them to the four schools as they arrived at the end of the road head. Problems would undoubtedly be encountered on a day-to-day basis, when technical advice would be needed. Reports would also need to be submitted to the district offices on the progress of the school rebuild.

A decision was made to engage two overseeing engineers on five-month contracts to live in the two areas NAFA had rebuild commitments. Sadit Maharjan, a slim, youthful-looking engineer from Kathmandu, was contracted for the four schools in the Tawal area, and played a critical role in supporting the first phase of the rebuild, ensuring both quality and efficiency in construction.

The role Sadit faced was daunting. The local population was in shock, struggling to recover from the destruction of all housing and community infrastructure, but determined to rebuild their communities with funding help from NAFA and like-minded foreign donors. Sadit had to supervise four building sites up to three hours' walk away, often having to return to far-away villages on consecutive days, depending on the urgency of engineering support required for specific building tasks.

Like Sabin, Sadit was enthusiastic to help but very aware of the gravity of the responsibility. The following are extracts from an article Sadit wrote for a NAFA newsletter on his experience of living in Tawal during the initial phase of the rebuild.

> "My will to help the earthquake-affected areas recover and the enthusiasm to be with needy people were my main motivation.
>
> While I was happy and pumped up with this wonderful opportunity, I was equally anxious. Moreover, I was very

> curious about the setting and the gargantuan task ahead. I came to know that the construction sites were situated in tough terrains of Ree VDC, in Dhading district. With limited skilled manpower, geographical hindrances for the transport of materials, and with no real mechanical equipment, it wasn't going to be easy by any means, but the existing conditions of the schools, the children, hopeful eyes of the people, and motivation from everyone around gave a huge boost to my confidence. I realized that I just had to do this."

Over the first phase of the rebuild, Sadit demonstrated a high level of engineering, communication and reporting skills, gaining great respect from villagers. Working with local builders unused to more modern building techniques made Sadit's task especially challenging.

> "The start was difficult, as most of the builders had never practised using cement. Furthermore, they were illiterate and had no understanding of earthquake-resilient design and dimensions. I remember cutting an 80-cm long stick in Latab just to demonstrate how wide and deep the trench was going to be."

Sadit strengthened local capacity, and was impressed with the local builders' attitude, efforts and capacity to learn.

> "The hardworking, dedicated, sincere and talented builders showed immense improvement over time. This assured good quality and precision in the classrooms built. I must say, except for the few adjustments as per the site conditions, the implementation of the overall design and specifications has been up to the mark. For the classroom blocks which are going to be built next

> year, I am confident that the builders are well equipped, with adequate knowledge and practice, and that they will be able to carry on this rebuilding even on their own. For me, this has been the greatest satisfaction."

The high standard of construction and the cost-effectiveness of the rebuild of the four Tawal-area schools owe a lot to Sadit's excellent engineering supervision and his capacity to engage with people in a manner that brought out the best in them. The experience also had a lasting impression on Sadit.

> "My stay in Tawal has been a whole new experience for me. Besides supervising construction, living a rural lifestyle, and learning Tamang language and cultures, I have also had the chance to witness firsthand the struggle and hardships of the people here. I have felt the patience of the men on the site who consistently worked, day in and out, and broke up the huge room-sized boulders manually. When I saw the sweat dripping off the people walking past me carrying loads twice their weight, I would forget my tiredness. One night in the village, outside the neighbour's house, I witnessed the pain of a mother giving birth right there on the ground, before one of the health workers could provide support and medical aid. I forgot the stinging pain in my feet.
>
> Despite such adversities, I also celebrated Lhosar and the five-day Manne festival, where everyone came together, forgetting the sorrows of their lives and sharing the joys...the amount of love and respect from the people here has driven me and has helped me persevere through the tough times. The rewards that my soul has received here are the moments I shall cherish all my life."

The rebuild was to be done in three phases, based on the seven-month local building seasons, themselves dependent upon when road access for bringing in building materials was possible: December 2016 to June 2017, November 2017 to June 2018 and December 2018 to February 2019. The number of phases was largely dependent on the availability of funds and the rate at which classrooms – and, in the case of Tawal, a new school toilet block – could be constructed each building season, given the limited pool of builders and competing demands on their time.

Classrooms were funded by NAFA and its donor partners according to the space needed for student enrolments. On average, the architect estimated, each classroom would cost approximately eight lakhs (AUD$10,000), nett of volunteer labour and reuse of building materials. This was double the cost of pre-earthquake classrooms. Local communities in all villages agreed to contribute significant volunteer work during the rebuild – constructing retaining walls, excavating and levelling the site for construction, making aggregate, carrying materials from the road head, and clearing the sites following construction. Tradesmen and their helpers were to be paid daily rates recommended by the government.

In the first phase, seventeen classrooms in four Dhading villages were rebuilt. In the second phase, another eighteen classrooms were rebuilt. With the rebuild supported by government-approved building plans, earthquake-resistant training of local builders and supervision by local engineers, we were confident that everyone had done their best to ensure construction of the strongest possible classrooms for the children and their teachers.

Coordinating the rebuild of schools in four villages was a massive task. Kanchha kept detailed records of construction costs in each village, helped by Sadit, the Rebuild Construction Committees in the four villages, and Social Mobiliser Dawa Tamang, who was funded by NAFA to support Sadit and Kanchha over the two rebuilding seasons. The HRDC financial records were audited in Dhading Bensi, with the financial statements then submitted to the District Level Project Implementation Unit, the authority responsible for overseeing the earthquake rebuild.

Rebuilding the four Ree VDC schools could not have happened without the drive and competence of Kanchha Tamang, President of the HRDC and a teacher at the Tawal school. Apart from Kanchha, credit for completing the largest school, the fifteen classroom Tawal-area school, goes to four builders: Sirap Tamang, Buddha Tamang, Kanchha Dong Tamang and Suk Lama Tamang. They kept the rebuild progressing in the face of competing demands from families to rebuild houses they had lost in the earthquake.

The government had offered villagers three lakhs (AUD$3,750) as compensation for homes destroyed by the earthquake, but only if they rebuilt the homes in accordance with the new earthquake-resistant standards. Builders and labourers trying to rebuild school classrooms were torn between family obligations and community responsibilities. A suggestion that builders may need extra incentive to keep their focus on the school rebuild was rejected by Kanchha. He was concerned about its impact on the budget and also thought it would create community division. So daily wages remained at government-recommended rates and the rebuild continued.

From the volunteer community, a few images and stories stand out. On many of our visits, we saw women sitting in groups, breaking up stones, using hammers and a rubber thong with a hole in it, to produce the aggregate needed for concrete. On another occasion, 150 volunteer villagers worked for thirteen hours in the rain to lay the roof slab for the eight-classroom, two-storey school block at Tawal.

For the villagers in the area, the Tawal hub school was their pride and joy. After its destruction in the earthquake, the school Principal, Sri Bahadur Tamang, expressed how much the school meant to them.

> "And it was the villagers' hard work and their labour freely given and in their collective agreement. The villagers rose up together to build this school. The stone blocks you see here, the wooden beams, the grounds, the fence, all of this, each and every piece was built by the villagers here. The school was built by their labour and their hard work and so the villagers feel a lot of love towards the school."

The school at Tawal had been built over nearly ten years in the lead-up to the earthquake. The three main builders of the school remembered that NAFA had to that point been able to fund only a classroom or two a year in the area. When they saw the school in ruins after the earthquake, they logically concluded that the school was unlikely to be rebuilt in their lifetime. A best-case scenario was perhaps fifteen to twenty years.

They did not foresee the generosity of people in Australia, Spain and Austria. In February 2019, eleven supporters of NAFA, ranging in age from sixteen to eighty-three, and the same number of supporters of Smile Back to Me arrived for the official handover of schools rebuilt in Kutal, Latab and Richet and the official opening of the school at Tawal.

The handover of the eight-classroom school block at Kutal was first up. I was the Chief Guest. During my handover speech, my eyes filled with tears as I acknowledged the difficult journey the local community had experienced since the earthquake. Eighteen people had died in a village comprising just 100 families. Richet was next, a three-hour walk from our campsite. I asked Raul, the driving force behind Smile Back to Me to be Chief Guest here, in acknowledgment of all he had done to help the area before and since the earthquake.

The following day, the group headed up to Latab, a ninety minute hike from Tawal for Westerners (less than sixty minutes for school students and other locals). Children from Latab walk to and from Tawal six days a week to attend school for Grades 6 to 10. Latab had been the base for distributing roofing sheets and rice for five weeks after the earthquake. As we stood on the site that had been cleared as a helipad, I told the group a few stories from the uplift adventure. I pointed to the large boulder that villagers sat on during the uplift as they watched helicopters approach the village from the valley below, and recounted the story of the small boy who tugged on my pant leg as a warning to sit down to avoid the downdraft. I had to hesitate while emotions welled up from within. I was slightly embarrassed by this outpouring of feelings nearly four years after the earthquake, but it was something I had difficulty controlling.

Villagers turned out in force for the handover at Latab. They had been involved from the initial response to the earthquake, and now it was time to celebrate the completion of their school rebuild. We sat with other guests and watched some of the children dance with enthusiasm and pride. They told us later that the choreography of a few of the more modern dance pieces had been learnt from YouTube. Deb and I held hands at one point and I told her in a low voice:

> "This is why we have been coming here for the past 15 years."

Deb was Chief Guest and gave her speech in Nepali to the quietest and most attentive Nepal village audience we have ever experienced! She then handed over the keys of another eight-classroom school block to a grateful Principal, Lok Tamang. Everyone again joined in and celebrated the handover with the traditional Tamang Mendho Maya dance.

On the eve of the official opening of the school at Tawal, Raul asked to have a quiet word with me. He had witnessed my emotions in Kutal and Latab and was concerned.

> "'Rod, I think you may be experiencing a form of post-traumatic stress. Maybe you should talk to a professional about it.'

> 'Thanks Raul—I couldn't believe I got upset again today – I thought enough time had passed. You may have a point. If I have trouble talking about the earthquake after all this time, imagine what the villagers must still be feeling. Maybe the opening ceremony tomorrow will help us all to move on. I just hope I can get through my speech without breaking down. If I continue to have trouble talking about the earthquake, I will see someone.'"

Finally, on 26 February 2019, the day arrived for the official opening of the fifteen classroom school at Tawal. Kanchha coordinated preparation of the opening and was the Master of Ceremonies for what turned out to be a six-hour event! The ceremony was scheduled to start late in the morning, giving the many politicians and senior bureaucrats time to travel by jeep from Dhading Bensi and beyond. Kanchha asked us to stay at our campsite until they were ready to start the opening ceremony. At 11 am, we were on our way to the school, a ten minute walk from our campsite. On the way, we crossed a small helipad that had been built since the earthquake but was now covered with large boulders that had come down in a landslide five months earlier, just as Professor Dhital had warned when he undertook the rapid assessment for landslide risk.

An estimated 1,200 villagers had arrived for the official opening and were seated or standing at every vantage point. As we approached the schoolgrounds, The Seekers' version of *I Am Australian* was playing. I had emailed Kanchha a link to the song a few months earlier, saying that the NAFA group would try to sing the song at the official opening. Students would start with the Nepali national anthem and we would follow with what we think should be Australia's national anthem, *I Am Australian*. Stephanie, a long-time NAFA supporter, and sixteen-year-old Eloise, the youngest member in the NAFA group, led us in the song to an appreciative audience.

Dances by local students were wonderful. A nationally acclaimed singer, Birnu Lama, had been invited to sing at the opening. As soon as he started his set, he was quickly surrounded by teenage boys and girls dancing up a storm. Kumar Tamang, from Latab and now being supported by NAFA and Smile Back to Me to study media communication in Dhading Bensi, followed with two songs he had recently performed in winning a national television singing competition. We were greatly impressed by his poise and his wonderful voice as he sang with pride in front of a local audience.

In amongst the dancing and singing, I handed over the keys to the rebuilt school and some computers donated to the school by NAFA.

There were too many speeches by local politicians and senior government officers. Each spoke without notes (one for twenty-six minutes). We know from summarised translations communicated to us later that they wanted to thank us for helping with the rebuild of the schools. We are unsure what else took up so much time, but certainly, a lot was said!

As the closing Chief Guest speaker, I waited (very) patiently for my turn. But as I listened to the politicians, I started to mentally amend the speech I had planned to make. I watched politician after politician speak, knowing that no government funds had gone into the rebuild of the four schools handed over during the visit. I looked forward to thanking local builders and volunteers for all the effort they had put in. I was conscious of my emotions, knowing that last-minute changes would complicate my delivery and wanting to get through my speech without incident, but nevertheless, I felt it necessary to give it a go.

So, when it was my time to speak, I first addressed the audience of villagers, teachers and students, stressing that their determination was the key factor that had made the new facilities possible. Then, I turned and spoke to the politicians and government officers sitting in a line amongst the invited guests. I implored them to better support and advocate for villages in the area. I stressed that working with the villagers had raised three priority needs: safety, health and education. I then identified three specific requests for government help:

- An engineer to assess the landslide that had occurred above the school five months previously and also to recommend further mitigating strategies in the likely event of further landslides in the area.
- Registration of the Tawal health post and allocation of a government-supported quota for one health-worker position there.
- Government provision of at least one more quota for a teacher salary at the Tawal school.

These were all requests for government support that the visiting Australians and Spanish took for granted back home. I was relieved to finish the speech without any emotional interventions. The traditional Mendho Maya dance, of course, followed. Everyone was smiling and celebrating. Kanchha looked so happy. He had been on such a difficult journey since the earthquake, and the weight was now being lifted off his shoulders. It was time for him to dance. The students, teachers and community now had a school that was better than before the earthquake, with more classrooms, built to earthquake-resistant building standards, a new school toilet block and new water taps. We had 'built back better'!

When the Mendho Maya was over, one of the politicians approached me and promised he would find a geotechnical engineer to come and undertake a landslide-risk assessment. The rest smiled, said goodbye, and got into their jeeps to return to Dhading Bensi. That evening, Raul and I stood together beside his tent, brushing our teeth before calling it a night. We would be returning to Kathmandu the next morning and were thrilled things had gone so well during the visit. I noticed that I would have just enough toothpaste to get back to Kathmandu and a fresh supply. Raul and I exchanged foamy grins.

> "Well, Raul, I can't imagine a better day. How good is it that so many of us could be here to share it?"
>
> Raul replied, "So good my friend, and I'm thinking we can all move on now and put the heartache behind us."
>
> Noting that Deb would not be impressed with the miniscule amount of toothpaste left, I nodded, "Yes, I think this is what's called closure."

Chapter 14

Beg saved my life and my baby's life

In planning the rebuild of community infrastructure in the aftermath of the earthquake, we had initially assumed the health post would be rebuilt within a similar timeframe as the school. Plans were drawn up for the new health post, and a fundraising campaign attracted generous donations from NAFA supporters. Fundraising activities included a 100-km hike in twenty-four hours by Ray Baker from adventure travel agency Back Track Adventures and a NAFA crowd-funding campaign.

But nearly four years later, construction had not commenced. Why? In retrospect, one component of the community development framework proved problematic – understanding the context. In the case of the rebuild of this important community asset, it was much more complex than we envisaged. The original health post was located on a terrace above the school. In his geotechnical assessment of Ree VDC villages for landslide risk, Professor Dhital concluded that there was a risk of landslide from the hills above the school and health post. He recommended that a fifty-metre-long by eight-metre-high gabion wall be built on the terrace where the health post was located. The health post was, however, too close to the hills above, so Professor Dhital suggested that it be rebuilt on another site, safe from the risk of landslides. It was to prove prophetic.

Three years later, towards the end of the monsoon season, a large landslide came down from the hills. Large boulders covered the helipad that had been built between Tawal village and the school.

Boulders, rocks and mud covered the site of the former health post, as well as our usual campsite for visits to the area. The gabion wall, constructed after the earthquake in accordance with Professor Dhital's design, stopped rocks and mud from tumbling and flowing onto the schoolgrounds.

An alternative, suitable site would need to be sourced before the health post could be rebuilt. It was to prove a difficult search. Unlike Australia, publicly owned land is not available in Nepali villages for community infrastructure. Land would need to be purchased from a farmer whose family had owned and planted crops on that block of land for generations.

In the immediate aftermath of the earthquake, the health post operated from a damaged but partially repaired church. However, by early 2016, the church wanted their building back for church activities. The health post was forced to move to a large US Aid tent. The tent was far from desirable, especially when the monsoon rains arrived in the middle of the year. When we visited the area in February and again in November 2017, the health post was still operating from the tent.

While the search for a farmer willing to sell his land continued, the HRDC, at our urging, began the process of registering the health post with the Nepal government. Until now, the health post had not been officially registered, although the government knew about it and in fact used it throughout the year to host government health workers for vaccination and baby clinics. Tawal was the most logical location for a health post in the VDC. It was the largest village in the area and a hub village for education and commerce.

In the face of ongoing delays securing land suitable for the health post, we pressured HRDC representatives for the health post to be moved from the tent to a multiroom complex at Meledanda, an area just below Tawal on the footpath to Kutal. This was the site for the second community-built school in the area. The complex had recently been constructed by the Nepal Army as emergency accommodation in the event of any future natural disasters in the area. Two of the rooms were currently being used as a ward office and a post office. It was agreed that two of the remaining rooms be taken over by the health post. Electricity was connected from the micro-hydro system, and some lockable cupboards, a hospital bed and a stretcher were replaced.

Unfortunately, all the patient records had been destroyed in the earthquake. Faced with the overwhelming challenge of simply staying open to provide basic health services, record-keeping of patient treatment stopped after the earthquake. Other records, such as staff attendance and the distribution of medicine, also stopped being kept, despite having been meticulously maintained prior to the earthquake. At least now, in the army-built rooms, the health post was again in dry premises, and we encouraged recommencement of the important task of record-keeping.

Finally, in February 2018, nearly three years after the earthquake, a suitable site for the new health post was found and purchased. The land was centrally located in Tawal village but was on multi-terraced land. A few of the terraces had to be flattened to make the site wide enough for the health post. Retaining walls had to be built on both the upper and lower boundaries. While that work was being done, I pressed the issue of registration. NAFA hoped registration would mean the eventual possibility that the government would take over responsibility for one or more health-worker salaries, which NAFA had been funding since 2002. Beg informed us that registration would also attract some free medicine, as well as small payments for each pregnancy, for both the health post and the mother.

But registration would turn out to be a very long, difficult and frustrating process. At first, health officials in the district headquarters, Dhading Bensi, insisted that the health post become a separate legal entity to its legal auspice up to that time, the HRDC. A company called Tawal Health Foundation was legally established. The broader term 'Foundation' was recommended to enable a range of primary and ancillary health services to operate from the health post. Then a PAN (tax) number was needed. The adoption of the new Nepali Constitution in September 2015 meant that responsibility for registration now involved the newly formed Ganga Jamuna Rural Municipality, of which Tawal and surrounding villages were a part.

Land for the health post had been purchased. But the three main builders in the area were busy completing construction of the new toilet block at the Tawal school and doing the finishing touches in the lead-up to the official opening ceremony in February 2019. With the health post now operating in dry, albeit temporary, premises, I told the HRDC that NAFA would transfer the rebuild funds only after the health post was registered. I also suggested that they try to negotiate a health-worker quota (salary) in exchange for NAFA's offer to rebuild the health post. Chandra and I judged that this was the time to try and force a reluctant government's hand.

In April 2019, Kanchha, health post coordinator Beg Tamang and elected Rural Municipality Ward representative Faising Tamang held a series of meetings with the elected president and chief administrator of the Ganga Jamuna Rural Municipality. Excuses were given by government officials as to why registration and the allocation of a government health-worker quota could not proceed at this time, including lack of patient data since the earthquake! During the discussions, the government officials advised that registration was not required to rebuild the health post.

I wanted to continue to force the issue with the government. But NAFA committee members were concerned about the ongoing delays, and the possible legal implications of not rebuilding the health post after conducting a public crowd-funding appeal. A decision was made to start the rebuild after the 2019 monsoon season, when roads to the area would reopen and building materials could be trucked in.

It was a frustrating time. Many generous NAFA supporters, including personal friends, had donated funds towards the rebuild of the health post and would be wondering why it was taking so long. First, it was the land issue. Second, it was access to the builders, who were focussed on completing the rebuild of the secondary school at Tawal. Third, it was the registration issue, and the implementation of a new national constitution that added a layer to the approval process – the Rural Municipality.

We were also frustrated with Beg, who had stopped maintaining detailed patient records. I could understand the constraints in the immediate aftermath of the earthquake, but Beg still seemed reluctant to recommence record-keeping three years later. He also seemed reluctant to pressure registration with the government. Why? In frustration, I even threatened to suspend his salary until the registration process was completed.

Finally, during our November 2019 visit, we discovered the reason for Beg's hesitation. In discussions with him translated by Bijaya, Beg asked if he and Lila Maya could do after-hours private work when the health post was eventually registered.

> "'But surely the government will formally appoint you as the coordinator of the health post following registration?' I asked."

Beg didn't think so.

> "I am too old to apply for a public-service position now, which is a prerequisite to applying for a permanent government position."

Suddenly, it hit home to us. It was likely the government would bring in a new health worker who had secured a permanent quota position elsewhere. This seemed unfair, as Beg was still young at forty-five and was well respected in the area. We later confirmed that in Nepal, if you are over thirty-five, you can't apply for a permanent position (quota) in the public service. This would be discriminatory under Australian law, and the laws of most Western countries, but it explained why Beg had been so hesitant about pushing the registration process.

It was also possible that Rural Municipality officers were hesitating to approve registration because of the existence of the government health post at Salleri, a forty-five minute walk from Tawal and even further away from other villages in the western part of the VDC. This health post, built at about the same time as the health post at Tawal, had in recent years improved the scope of its services. It now had a birthing centre, and while Beg still does some blood and urine testing in the Tawal health post, more sophisticated equipment is based at the Salleri health post, where there is also a lab and a lab technician.

Baby clinics and vaccinations are often organised by health workers based at the Salleri health post, though these clinics are usually also conducted in Tawal. Beg estimates that 50% of babies are born at home and 50% at the Salleri birthing room. He says mothers prefer to have their baby at home and fear caesareans. Health workers from Salleri come to Tawal to see expectant mothers. They estimate delivery dates, encouraging mothers to come to Salleri a few days before the expected due date.

Nevertheless, Tawal is the largest village in the area and, until the earthquake, was the 'go to' health post in the area. All three health workers are now very experienced, and are well respected and trusted in the community. The earthquake destroyed a perfectly functional health post facility, and while there is no doubt that the service provided out of the US Aid tent was not to the previous standard, Beg estimated that the health post still treated over 2,000 patients a year, with approximately 50% seen as in-home patients. The health workers had saved many lives over the years, especially in the immediate aftermath of the earthquake. They had also safely delivered many babies.

The story of Manju and her baby is one such example. Bijaya, Deb and I met Manju in November 2019. She lives in Tawal Bensi and her baby, Malika, had been born eight months previously. Manju told us:

> "Beg saved my life and my baby's life."

She told us she had experienced severe stomach pain from 8 pm on the evening before her baby was born. The pain turned out to be a urinary blockage, and at 1 am, Beg was called up from his home in Kutal. Beg said Manju's screams of pain could be heard throughout the village. He was able to release the urinary blockage. Manju said that had it gone on for ten more minutes, she would have died, and she hopes no-one else ever suffers the agony she did that night.

A second life-threatening problem was that the umbilical cord was wrapped around the unborn baby's neck. Although Beg was able to unwrap the cord, the baby was barely alive when born. After being held by the mother-in-law, baby Malika was revived and now lay in Manju's arms, smiling up at us. After meeting with Manju, we asked if any mothers or babies had died in childbirth since the health post opened in 2002. Beg confirmed there had been no deaths during that time.

Construction of the new health post was commenced in January 2020. Steady progress was made until a government lockdown associated with COVID-19 (see Postscript) caused a delay in builders and labourers being able to work as a group on the project. Then the annual monsoon rains closed the roads leading into the area. Building materials needed for the health post toilet block couldn't be brought in from Dhading Bensi, and so the health post remained in Meledanda. When the roads opened again in early October, work continued. The rebuilt health post finally became operational in early 2021, nearly six years after being destroyed by the earthquake! A year later, Beg and Lila Maya continue to be the health workers, with their salaries paid by NAFA. The health post remains unregistered.

Chapter 15

Tooth-brushing after tiffin

While we were grappling with the health post registration issue, an opportunity arose to address another long-identified community health problem. As far back as our January 2011 visit, Beg had raised the need for a local dental camp, telling us a dentist had never visited the area. Obviously, addressing this vital health issue would need to involve a combined preventative and curative oral program. It would be seven years before we could establish the connections to make this plan a reality.

Poor oral health is prevalent in rural Nepal, including the Tawal area. This is the result of inadequate community awareness of good oral-health practices (such as tooth-brushing techniques and using fluoride toothpaste), the shortage of dental services, especially outside the cities, and dietary changes. The traditional diet of millet, wild foods and locally grown vegetables was generally good for oral health. However, food-consumption habits began to change when the road was extended closer to the village during the dry season. Local shops began bringing in more processed foods, sweets, sugary drinks and salty snacks.

The nearest dental service was in the district headquarters, Dhading Bensi. There are no public oral-health services in Nepal, so dental care was expensive and most subsistence farmers did not have the disposable income to pay for it. It was clear that an oral-health public assessment, awareness and treatment program could markedly improve the oral-health knowledge and practices of villagers, which would also improve their overall health.

In November 2014, we had met with Dr Buddhi Man Shrestha, Director of the Kantipur Dental College Teaching Hospital and Research Centre, to discuss the feasibility of an oral-health program for Tawal and nearby villages. The Centre's submission to NAFA for funding to support a baseline survey of oral-health status in the Tawal area emphasised the importance of oral health and its link with general health outcomes.

> "Oral health is fundamental to general health and wellbeing, significantly impacting on quality of life. It can also affect general health conditions…The main factors controlling the risk of dental caries (cavities) are oral hygiene, exposure to fluoride and a moderate frequency of consumption of cariogenic foods.
>
> More than 57% of Nepalese children at six years of age and 69% of adults above the age of 50 suffer from untreated dental caries affecting more than three teeth. Untreated dental caries is the most prevalent childhood disease in Nepal – more prevalent than malnutrition (53%) and vitamin deficiency (58%)…Tooth decay is one of the most common chronic childhood diseases."

A four-day combined baseline-assessment survey and curative dental camp had been scheduled to commence on 26 April 2015, but the Gorkha earthquake struck the day before, forcing cancellation of the camp. We then had to wait until February 2017, when the community was back on its feet, before the inaugural camp could be rescheduled.

The HRDC promoted the camp throughout the area. The dental team for the four-day program was led by Dr Smita Dhakal and comprised five female Nepali dentists. The first dental camp ever conducted in Ree VDC, it included oral-health screening, oral hygiene instruction, simple extractions and fillings. Toothpaste and toothbrushes donated to NAFA and brought over from Australia were also distributed. A World Health Organization (WHO) questionnaire used to obtain data for the baseline survey proved long and cumbersome, taking up too much of the dentists' time.

A total of 208 villagers – 143 females (69%) and sixty-five males (31%) attended the camp, with only five assessed as having good oral health! Over the four days, the dentists performed thirty-six tooth extractions and four restorations (fillings). A summary of camp findings was prepared by a member of the Kantipur Dental Hospital team. Not surprisingly, the most common findings were the prevalence of cavities, gum disease, infections, and missing teeth due to cavities.

Comments in the summary reflected the major challenges ahead for the program:

> "Most of them had Dental Caries (cavities) as major oral disease. Due to lack of oral health awareness, patients opted for removal of tooth once they get dental decay, instead of treating their tooth on time and saving them … Also, most people had no habit of regular brushing. Our team distributed toothbrushes and toothpastes. We also demonstrated the tooth-brushing techniques. With enforcement of knowledge through oral hygiene instruction, our team hopes the oral hygiene gets better when we visit there for next time."

After the dental camp, we met again with Dr Buddhi Man to discuss the findings of the baseline survey and options for further camps. Dr Buddhi Man proposed a five-year curative, preventative and educational oral-health program. A key component of the program would be promotion of good oral-health practices. A representative

Action Group would be formed, and trained to take ownership and responsibility for sustaining the program between the annual dental camps. Dietary change and regular tooth-brushing with fluoride toothpaste would be promoted through the local Action Group and through the local health workers.

There would be a focus on schoolchildren, who would in turn take improved oral-health practices back to their families. A tooth-brushing program would be set up for schoolchildren from Nursery to Grade 3. Toothbrushes would be kept at the school and stored in the classroom in cloth toothbrush holders made by local women tailors. The annual dental camps would include scaling, fluoride application, fillings and simple extractions.

A second oral and general health camp was held in April 2018. Before the dental team and medical officer arrived, the NAFA team, comprising myself, Deb, Bijaya and his wife, Binu, briefed community leaders on the program. We proposed that the Action Group comprise: elected leaders (including the Municipality Vice President, the Ward President, the women's representative and a lower-caste metalworker/Dalit representative); local health workers; the Women's Social Mobiliser (more on that position in Chapter 18); a Mothers' Group representative; the President of the HRDC and Agricultural Cooperative; a shopkeeper; the nursery teacher; three pastors; and the local Lama. We also encouraged approximately 200 parishioners, who attended three Saturday morning church services, to participate actively in the program.

In all, 276 villagers were assessed by the dental team, including forty-eight children screened on the second day when two dentists walked an hour and a half up to the village of Latab. Only six of those screened were assessed as having good oral health. Dental treatments provided included 37 extractions, 33 fluoride treatments, and 56 fillings. A PowerPoint presentation by the dentists to about 200 villagers in the central square at Tawal focussed on the causes of tooth decay, including diet, and on proper tooth-brushing technique.

A third oral and general health camp was held in February 2019. A total of 265 (60% female and 40% male) patients were examined. An oral hygiene instruction and awareness program was carried out among the villagers and the students from Grades 1 to 4 at the Tawal school. The number of dental problems in adults who were examined and treated followed a similar pattern as at previous camps.

> "Among the total participants, 478 teeth were found to be decayed, 92 teeth were found to be missing due to cavities and 12 teeth were found to have fillings."

There were, however, more encouraging findings in a survey of children undertaken during the camp, as evidenced in the table below.

Kantipur survey of children in 2019 dental camp

Survey issue	Answer	Frequency (Number)	Percentage (%)
Presence of dental problems	Yes	42	65
	No	23	35
	Total	65	100
Knowledge on sugar causing tooth decay	Yes	39	60
	No	26	40
	Total	65	100
Times of brushing	Once	35	54
	Twice	28	43
	Never	2	3
	Total	65	100

The tooth-brushing program in the school seemed to be working. The overall oral hygiene among examined children was also more promising.

Variable	Frequency (Number)	Percentage (%)
Good	32	49.20
Fair	25	38.50
Poor	8	12.30
Total	65	100.00

But over the three dental camps to that point, the outcomes for older students and adults were not as successful. We agreed with the Kantipur Dental Hospital view that the number of older students and adults presenting at the camp for a check-up should have been higher.

> "We believe that the organizing committee and the volunteers certainly expected a lot more attendance in our dental camp. Many of the villagers seemed less concerned about their oral health... Patients whose awareness is non-existent will only request treatment when pain is present, and pain is only present during acute phases... Then the symptoms change, pain disappears, and the pathology/infection can continue to evolve... Through these chronic phases, patients often don't feel anything and therefore do not consider they need treatment."

The dentists also gave a second PowerPoint presentation in the central square of Tawal village one evening, but there were fewer attendees than the previous year. We had provided feedback that the PowerPoint presentation the year before had been overly detailed, with too many slides on extreme oral diseases and not enough focus on prevention. While some adjustments had been made, the presentation was still too complex, a concern confirmed by feedback from community leaders. We shared that feedback with the Kantipur Dental Hospital team and appreciated the acknowledgement in their summary report on the third camp that the preventative components of the dental camps needed to be improved.

> "In our past programs, our preventive programs have been focussed on providing PowerPoint presentations and demonstrations using charts and models. However, due to reduced number of participants, maybe this approach needs to be modified. As pointed out to us by the people, the presentations might have been too technical, and the students might have lost interest in the process.
>
> We need to carry out health education programs in a more student friendly and innovative manner. Rather than curative, we plan to prioritize preventive and awareness programs for our next visit. We want to have more interactive sessions with the children and their parents, design games related to oral health, make catchy jingles and songs for the children to remember. We hope we can meet our shortcomings in future [dental camps]."

At the fourth dental camp, conducted from 4 February to 7 February 2020, a total of 248 villagers from four local villages were examined. Forty-three of them were adults, but the majority (a total of 205) were children – fifty-four who were brought to the camp from the school at Latap, fifty from the school at Kutal and 101 from the school at Dhuseni. Of the villagers examined, 236 received treatment, with 84 extractions, 82 fillings and 70 scalings performed.

The tooth-brushing program directed at children in their early school years has been a successful component of the oral-health program, with the oral health of local children continuing to demonstrate encouraging progress. It was particularly heartening during our visit to see groups of smiling children brushing their teeth at the school water taps after eating their 'tiffin' (lunch).

However, once again, fewer adults than anticipated attended the dental camp. It seems the Action Group was not an effective mechanism for encouraging adult participation in the program. Community mobilisation had been an important factor in constructing the micro-hydroelectricity system, establishing the agricultural cooperative, and surviving and rebuilding after the earthquake. But the same level of community mobilisation was not evident in regard to this important health issue. There are several possible reasons for this. Firstly, the composition of the Action Group was suggested by us during our visit rather than having been built on existing lines of communication. The HRDC was there, but we had observed that this was not an effective information-sharing mechanism when it came to including women.

Secondly, it seemed that the Social Mobiliser had deferred to the elected Ward Representative, who was nominated through that position of authority to be Chairperson of the Action Group. The Social Mobiliser left the organising of Action Group meetings to the Chairperson, and this did not happen. In our view, the inactivity of the Action Group was a major reason for the poor adult buy-in to the program, along with the villagers' prevailing attitude that adults go to dentists only when they have a specific problem with their teeth.

Having said that, though, the program was achieving positive results, particularly for young children, and it is hoped this next generation will be more aware of good oral-health practices.

Chapter 16

No house, no work, no livelihood

From the very beginning of our contact with the HRDC, Deb would ask, "Where are the women?" Few elected women representatives appeared at meetings. Deb's queries were always met with reassurances that women had been invited but were busy elsewhere with their duties. Working with women, one of the most disadvantaged groups in developing countries, is a key part of community development. Addressing women's inequality in society was one of the UN Millennium Development Goals. We were usually in the area towards the end of the harvesting season, so women were busy. But we still wondered how we could better engage with them.

NAFA's earliest projects focussed on community-wide water infrastructure, education and health. These all benefited women and girls but were not specifically targeting them. At that stage, we had not found a way to include women in consultation and negotiation processes. In November 2008, the HRDC requested NAFA's support to establish a women's literacy program in the area. We were excited that the women themselves had approached the HRDC about this, and we asked that they meet with us in the monastery that evening to develop a proposal.

We stumbled into the dark monastery, blinking at small pinpricks of light until our eyes adjusted to see thirty expectant faces looking up at us, illuminated by small, hand-held Chinese lamps. The women had come out in force on a dark, cold night to put their case, and it was clear they regarded literacy as their highest development priority.

There are compelling reasons to invest time, energy and money in educating and empowering young girls and women. The knowledge, skills and self-confidence obtained boosts women's chances of earning an income through employment, improves the health of families, increases women's participation in society and accelerates their countries' transition to stable population growth. Functional literacy and the social dimension of literacy are also considered important for individual and community development by organisations such as UNESCO.

> "... the social dimension of literacy: 'creating literate environments and societies is essential for achieving the goals of eradicating poverty, reducing child mortality, curbing population growth, achieving gender equality and ensuring sustainable development, peace and democracy'."

In early 2009, NAFA funded an eight-month women's literacy course in Tawal and three nearby villages. Cheap solar lights were installed in the monasteries at Tawal and Dhuseni and at schools in Latab and Salleri. NAFA paid the part-time salaries of four teachers for the women's literacy course. This was the beginning of working more closely with women to meet their specific needs. It was also recognition that community development required attention to the needs of the wider geographical area, not just the village of Tawal.

Within a year, Chandra advised that the government was now providing teachers for women's literacy in the Ree VDC, meaning NAFA no longer needed to fund the classes. However, in November 2011, at a meeting with women at Tawal to obtain an update on their development priorities, the need for women's literacy classes was raised again. We were told that the government-run classes had not been successful, with teachers appointed from outside the area not turning up for classes. When they did show up, the women said, the teaching was of poor quality. Women again regarded literacy as their development priority.

Meanwhile the findings of a 2011 'Social Survey of Tawal' reinforced that underutilisation of women's skills and a lack of local markets for any products they might make were major barriers to income-earning opportunities. The survey's findings, together with the women's express desire for improved literacy, led NAFA to allocate funds for a second women's literacy program.

During our visits we witnessed the women's engagement with the program. In the very early hours of a winter morning, with mist still clinging to the treetops, we would hear from our tents the soft chatter and laughter of the women making their way to their literacy class. Deb roused herself from her sleeping bag to observe a lesson:

> "In the classroom, 20 women were sitting at the desks, many with a small child or a baby on their back. Yuna, the teacher, was writing out letters of the Nepali alphabet. She engaged the class by inviting individuals to write words on the whiteboard. The women laughed and encouraged each other. It was chilly outside, but in here it was warm and companionable. Snuggled against their mothers, the babies and toddlers slumbered on."

An evaluation of the second women's literacy program found that fifty women were enrolled in two classes – twenty in the basic class and thirty in the advanced class – including a small number of Dalit women (more about the Dalit families in Chapter 19). The average age of participants was twenty-six. Few women had been given the opportunity to gain an education. Approximately 70% had never attended school and those who had attended had not gone beyond

Grade 3. Two-thirds of the women said access to the women's literacy program had improved their literacy skills. Overall, the basic group was reading and writing at Grade 2 to 4 levels, the advanced group at Grade 4 to 5 levels.

The women said the main reason they wanted to improve their literacy was so they could undertake income-producing activities such as tailoring. They also wanted to be more active in improving their community and helping their children to study. The findings of the evaluation are consistent with other studies on the motivation of women attending women's literacy classes.

The specific economic interests of women were paramount again in the community-wide micro-hydro project. Women received government-funded training in making bamboo products (pencil holders, frames, coasters and so on) as a social enterprise. However, this project ceased when the Kathmandu-based trainer did not deliver on his promise of a market for the goods. This was a disappointing setback.

Deb continued to meet with women during our visits to the area. Their common development priority was a need for income-producing activities to supplement subsistence farming, but this was easier discussed than achieved. We were aware that skills training for the sake of it can be counterproductive. For example, women explained how some years ago, pickle-making training at Rigaun village led to a surplus of pickles they could neither consume nor sell. The training, though a pleasant diversion from normal activities, took them away from farming and earned them no cash, as there was no outside market for the pickles.

The problem of finding a market for products remained unresolved. Neither village women nor HRDC leaders or NAFA members had the time or contacts to invest in finding markets for as-yet-unidentified products. This is a major problem in economic development worldwide. Many an NGO has a surplus of beautiful handmade wooden carvings, weavings and craft products awaiting buyers. NAFA put women's income-generation on the back burner while forging ahead with broader community projects, all of which benefited women.

In 2012, access to electricity provided small-business opportunities for women, with one woman opening a beauty parlour and another setting up a poultry-butchering business. The following year, 100 female members of the newly established Pasang Chowk Agricultural Cooperative benefited from exposure to new farming techniques and crops. That same year, women were again centre stage, assessing the feasibility of improved cooking stoves and implementing the stoves on a trial basis across the Ree VDC.

Until 2015, incremental improvements had been made addressing women's health and educational needs. However, women's involvement had to be sought, even insisted upon. For example, during the week-long training program associated with the introduction of smoke-free stoves into the area, Deb realised that the training was focussing only on the installation of the stoves by men. Women as a group had not been invited to attend a session on the benefits and maintenance of the stoves. A session had to be quickly arranged, as the training program was nearing its end.

The Gorkha earthquake of 2015 was a turning point in addressing women's needs. Women were affected in particular ways by the natural disaster. NAFA members had an initial insight into women's needs through a rapid survey designed by women leaders of the Nepalese Association of Queensland (NAQ). The survey was conducted by Tawal leaders, with results intending to feed into a Brisbane-based seminar on disaster relief. Tawal women identified the following as their most pressing concerns:

- A lack of basic facilities (housing, clean water, toilets) and difficulties in carrying out daily household tasks and childcare.
- Depression, fear and anxiety from the earthquake and subsequent landslide risk.
- A need for skills development.

Kalpana Kaphle, a Brisbane-based social worker, gave a paper on trauma recovery at the NAQ workshop. She offered to come to Tawal with us in November 2015 to conduct trauma-recovery workshops with school students. Deb and Kalpana also intended to meet with the women, investigate their needs more fully and develop a plan of action. As it happened, the meeting took place impromptu when a handful of women lingered after a school committee meeting at which we had been onlookers. We began talking with the women informally and word soon spread that a 'meeting' for women was taking place. Within minutes, there was barely standing room in the broken-down classroom. More than 100 women of all ages, from high-school students to the oldest dressed in their swathes of cloth skirts and waist wraps, crowded in. The air was electric with expectation, and that expectation was squarely aimed at Deb, Kalpana and their helpers, Yuna and Sabita.

Kalpana is an experienced facilitator and was able to fully engage with the large group, using familiar Nepali idioms and Nepali humour to encourage two-way communication. Soon laughter echoed around the room. Deb was aware it was late in the day and knew the women would be hungry. When Santa, one of the men at the school committee meeting walked past, Deb asked if he could go to the village shops to buy "as many packets of biscuits as 1,000 rupees will buy" (the only money in her pocket).

The women's comments about their circumstances came thick and fast, echoing concerns found in the survey conducted soon after the earthquake. The women told of their fear of further landslides:

> "'We are afraid to go out of our shelter.'
>
> 'We feel tremors in the middle of the night and think this time we will die. Are we safe or not?'
>
> 'We feel we are standing still. We cannot start to make clean water, toilet, light again, as we do not know if it safe to rebuild in this place or we have to find a new place to live.'"

Everyday life was harder:

> "Everything is difficult now – looking after children, collecting wood, broken paths, no light, one communal toilet."
>
> "We are much more sick than before."

There was no embarrassment about discussing personal health matters:

> "I have not had a period for six months."
>
> "I have excessive bleeding, sometimes for over one month."
>
> "I have constant headaches, feeling stress and fear."

We checked with the larger group and found that more than half had experienced excessive bleeding in the past months and many said their period had stopped for many months. Over half also said they felt 'tingling in hands and legs', suggesting some nerve damage from back and limb injuries sustained in the earthquake. Many said they found sitting making dokos now gave them severe backache.

The women made suggestions for improving their situation such as skills training in sewing, animal-rearing or "any activity at all to earn some income to help our families". They felt having some income would help relieve tension and fear.

One woman summed up the situation:

> "No house, no work, no livelihood."

Halfway through the meeting, Santa came running up to the classroom, laden with an armload of biscuits and some tin plates, which we hastily loaded up and passed around. By this time the room was buzzing with laughter and chatter as the women exchanged stories and experiences related to their living conditions. Kalpana drew their attention back to the issues at hand by announcing that NAFA had just made some significant progress on safety concerns.

We told them that Professor Meg Dhital, a geotechnical engineer from Tribhuvan University, would be coming in two days' time to do a rapid assessment of the area for landslide risk. This good news prompted a round of applause, a rare event in meetings we had attended over the years. We then agreed on a plan of action. Health workers Sunita and Lila Maya would do a survey of women to gain specific information for a proposed gynaecological clinic, subject to the availability of funding. We would talk to Kanchha about income-producing opportunities, and training for women through the Pasang Chowk Agricultural Cooperative, as well as seeking a funding source for training programs in sewing and animal-rearing.

Deb was humbled by the women's 'can do' attitude, and their willingness to 'do what it takes' to rebuild livelihoods, asking only for a hand up to start the process of recovery. In the photo taken of the large group after the meeting, expectant faces look to the camera, the air of optimism shining through.

Due to the enormity of the fundraising effort for NAFA's rebuild program, private funding was sourced for a female-health camp run by female Nepali gynaecologists and organised by Beg, Lila Maya and Sunita. The actual camp proved extremely difficult to organise. Few medical specialists were keen to conduct a camp in such a remote village. It was also difficult to identify a suitable venue for the health camp, the earthquake having destroyed potential options and making the area a difficult place to work for doctors used to city conditions. A free two-day gynaecological camp was finally held on 20 March and 21 March 2018. A Dhading Bensi-based gynaecologist, two nurses and a pharmacist conducted the camp, with ninety-four women attending.

Meanwhile, we continued to grapple with the more complex and intractable problem of pursuing income-producing activities and seeking markets for products. Given that we already had, as a starting point, village women's involvement in the Agricultural Cooperative, we thought we could run a pilot 'developed' goat-rearing project. This activity had a proven market demand and was therefore likely to succeed. The pilot project proposed that ten of the poorest women who had some experience and an interest in goat-rearing would each receive training and a high-value 'Jamunapari' goat. The Jamunapari were new goats being introduced to the area. They were significantly larger than the local goats and were distinguished by their long ears.

NAFA included the goat proposal in an application to the English Family Foundation aimed at partnering to re-establish the Agricultural Cooperative after the earthquake. The application was successful, and our subsequent data collection and an evaluation of the pilot program have demonstrated that women have successfully raised and sold goats at a good profit. The pilot scheme has also been expanded, with distribution of the first baby she-goat to another impoverished woman member of the Cooperative, in accordance with the conditions of participation in the program.

Women had long been enthusiastic about learning sewing skills. They wanted to make their own clothes, such as school uniforms and men's clothing, which at the time had to be purchased in the district capital, Dhading Bensi. Many hoped to also sell to others from nearby villages, who came to Tawal, the largest village in the VDC, to shop on Saturdays.

We had concerns about the availability of markets for the tailored products. We hesitated to seek funds to train numerous women in sewing if they had only each other to buy the tailored products. We discussed the issue with the HRDC and women's group. The women informed us there were already three women tailors in Tawal, but they had more customers than they could handle. Other villages in the area had no tailors. They believed there would be enough demand for sewing work within the area and that training would provide opportunities for more women to set up small businesses.

An earmarked donation for a six-month tailoring program was received from Queensford College, a vocational training institute in Brisbane whose directors included members of Brisbane's Nepalese community. A master tailor was contracted from Dhading Bensi to conduct an on-site tailoring program for ten women with an interest in sewing. NAFA would also offer to contribute 50% of the cost of ten sewing machines, with the women contributing the other 50%. While applications for participation in the Jamunapari goat program were considered by the Cooperative, applications for participation in the tailoring program were considered by the HRDC.

In our November 2016 visit to Tawal, we observed the completion of the sewing training program. We were surprised to find that the trainer was conducting two sessions per day, one in the morning and one in the afternoon, enabling twenty women to be trained, sharing the ten sewing machines. The HRDC proposed this arrangement due to the large number of women requesting training and agreement by the master tailor to conduct the training for both a morning and an afternoon group. The HRDC reasoned that some women would set up businesses, while others would have skills to sew for their own families and could borrow a machine for that purpose.

The program was evaluated by Deb and two social-work students during our visit. For most of the women participating, it was their first small-business venture. The tailoring program had included instruction on patternmaking. Fortunately, the women's literacy course years before had improved their capacity to read. Overall, the participants' enthusiasm was palpable as they showed off the pleated school uniform skirts and traditional Nepali baby bonnets they made.

Some women were happy to make school uniforms for their children and clothing for their family and sell locally where possible. Others wanted to increase their cash income and sell to an outside market. In the evaluation, it became apparent that there was little understanding of some of the skills needed in running a small business. Not surprisingly, the evaluation report included the recommendation:

> "Explore the possibility of conducting a small-business training program to assist participants to learn more about the business side of tailoring."

We had anticipated this issue would arise, so I came prepared to facilitate, with the help of a translator, an information session on the 'business side of tailoring'. In Brisbane before the trip, I supplemented my knowledge of business practice with tailoring cost templates provided by another NAFA supporter who had years of experience in what he respectfully referred to as 'the rag trade'. At the information session, we discussed questions such as:

- How will you decide what garment to make?
- Who will buy the garments and where are the buyers located?
- How will you calculate the cost of making the garment and what price will you sell the garment for?

Lack of understanding of suitable market outlets became apparent in our discussions with the women. They asked if the Tamang-style clothing being made at the time would sell well in Australia. From our experiences selling Nepalese goods through NAFA's fundraising market stalls, we knew that specific ethnic clothing would be difficult to sell. Deb handed around two *Women's Weekly* magazines, which provided a visual 'crash course' on clothing in Australia. The women, wide-eyed and incredulous, scanned the pages.

Twenty women completed sewing training at the end of 2016 and ten purchased machines. Two women set up sewing businesses in Dhuseni, one at Latab and the remaining seven in Tawal. NAFA had made a solid start in addressing the specific needs and priorities of women post-earthquake, with encouraging signs of success. However, there was room to develop additional strategies to address the needs and expand economic opportunities for women in the area.

Deb believed a local 'mobiliser' was needed to encourage the identification of those new opportunities. During our visits, women were active, yet there was seemingly little progress between NAFA visits. Leadership was required to bring women together to discuss other ideas for training and to support one another. Deb's communication about women's activities went via Kanchha Tamang, the President of both the HRDC and the Cooperative. However, Kanchha was overseeing the earthquake-recovery program and was already stretched to the limit with those duties. Someone else was needed to monitor and expand the goat program, identify and assess the feasibility of producing and marketing handmade products, and generate other innovative ideas that would increase cash income for local women.

Back in Brisbane, Deb came up with two ideas. One was to fund a part-time Women's Social Mobiliser position to work with women year-round on expanding their opportunities. The other idea arose out of discussion with another NAFA member, Wendy Eastwell. Wendy wondered if the women could make reusable grocery bags to be sold locally in villages or back in Brisbane. At the time, the state of Queensland, like much of Australia, was moving to eliminate plastic bag use. Hopefully, cloth bags would be in demand. The logistics would need to be thought through, but the idea could at least be trialled.

Kanchha welcomed the proposal for a Women's Social Mobiliser position and consulted with the HRDC and women leaders. It was agreed that the part-time position would be advertised widely, with Grade 12 completion a minimum requirement. The job description set out the key duties and expected outcomes, as well as the salary and a budget for domestic travel.

Key duties were to:

- Develop ideas and strategies to increase women's employment opportunities in the villages of Tawal, Dhuseni, Latap, Kutal, Tawal Bensi, and Salleri.

- Monitor and evaluate existing health, education, women's tailoring and women's goat-rearing programs, as well as the benefits for women of membership in the Pasang Chowk Agricultural Cooperative.
- Liaise with key community members regarding women's needs and their interest in community-wide issues, including a proposed women's forum on health and the environment – menstrual management, environmental issues concerning disposal of women's sanitary pads, rubbish disposal, and women's input into crop-diversification (including fruit-tree growing) and reforestation strategies.
- Travel to Dhading Bensi and/or Kathmandu to explore skills-training resources for women's development.
- Explore potential outlets for locally made products.
- Meet fortnightly with Kanchha for supervision/guidance, and provide a brief fortnightly report to Deb based on a project diary (hours worked, activities undertaken, expenses incurred, etc).

Three women were shortlisted for the position. To guard against nepotism, the HRDC had applicants anonymously complete a written suitability test that was assessed by a panel. The successful applicant was Rebika Lama Tamang, a young woman who had lived away from Tawal for many years and had recently returned with her family. She spoke reasonable English, had passed Grade 12, and had work experience in a bank. We would meet Rebika for the first time in November 2017.

Meanwhile, on the sewing front, Wendy and Deb got to work designing and testing what they initially envisaged would be a shopping bag but would ultimately end up as a general-purpose tote bag. The first two attempts were comically too long and then too wide, but the third attempt was exactly right. We intended to pay the women fair-trade wages and purchase suitable material on advice from staff at Amrita Craft in Kathmandu, whose owner was a long-time supporter of NAFA.

The first visit to Tawal after the appointment of the Women's Social Mobiliser was extremely busy. Deb met Rebika and started work immediately, identifying tasks and organising the tote-bag initiative. The process of learning to make the bags involved a great deal of anxiety and fun. With Deb's limited Nepali, Rebika's limited knowledge of sewing, much use of facial and hand expressions and visual props, they managed to convey to the women the twelve-step process of making the bags.

Por Maya Tamang, an experienced tailor, made the first bag – it was well sewn but way too narrow. Wary of the material fraying, the women had made very wide seams, not needed for this material. This was corrected, resulting in well-sewn sample bags. The next task was to cut up 200 metres of fabric from giant rolls, enough for an initial run of 200 bags. However, Deb had not thought through the logistics. The only usable space was the monastery, with gaping holes in the walls caused by the earthquake, countless chickens running in and out, and a dusty carpet hiding uneven floorboards. On their hands and knees, Deb and the women started cutting out the 200 bags with enormous shear-like scissors on the wavy sea of wood. Seeing how long this was going to take, Por Maya kindly offered to take the material home and finish the cutting herself. On our next visit from Australia, we brought two bifold plastic tables and tailoring scissors to make the cutting process a little easier.

Quality control turned out, not unsurprisingly, to be problematic. The women had trouble with the straps. In the first batch, 40% of the bags had twisted straps, which had to be mended by Deb back in Australia. Finally, after several attempts at employing a woman to check the bags, one experienced tailor was successful in sending them back to the maker to be corrected. Deb was surprised to learn that some women did not like to be told to fix mistakes, making it difficult for the 'quality controller'.

Raul from Smile Back to Me, who usually joins us for our annual visits to the Tawal area, offered to buy some bags and take them back to Spain for sale. But the model of making tote bags in Nepal for sale in Australia or Spain was not ideal. To save freight costs, we were sending them back within the baggage allowances of NAFA supporters, but this became a challenge when the number of bags being made increased from 200 to 400 a year later.

Currently, Deb also makes the tags for the tote bags, orders material ahead of visits, irons the bags when they are back in Australia, and sells the bags through NAFA networks and, at this stage, one commercial outlet – a local fruit and vegetable shop. The model needs to change to be sustainable. We need to reach a point where the local women order and pay for the material and accessories in Kathmandu, organise transport of the materials up to Tawal, distribute the materials to women in nearby villages, make the bags, adhere to a quality-control system, organise transport of the tote bags and other handmade products to Kathmandu for sale in shops that cater mainly for tourists, and collect the sales proceeds. That's a lot of steps to profit from a tote bag!

Deb has started the process of training a lead tailor to come to Kathmandu, buy the accessories and meet with staff from Amrita Craft, a high-quality, fixed-price shop in Thamel, the tourist area of Kathmandu. Amrita Craft has years of experience marketing craft items in Nepal and overseas, and NAFA has a long association with the shop. Deb buys the material for the tote bags there. The shop's original owner, Mr Yagya Narayan Gupta, was a board member of the Joy Foundation Nepal. Sadly, Mr Gupta and other family members died in the April 2015 earthquake after his house in Kathmandu collapsed. His son, Ananta, now running the shop, has continued his father's strong support for NAFA and income-earning opportunities for women.

Deb and Wendy hoped that the tote bags could be sold through Amrita Craft. However, because fair-trade wages were being paid for the sewing, we soon discovered we could not compete with the price of bags made in Kathmandu. This was unfortunate, as it meant tailors in Tawal would need to decide whether they were prepared to accept a lower, piece-meal rate for their items and, hopefully, make up the lower profit margin through higher sales volume. Alternatively, we could try bringing them back to Australia to sell. We decided to do the latter. As sending them by freight or post was assumed to be costly, either we or other NAFA supporters had to bring back the tote bags (and later aprons) as personal luggage, a very logistically challenging process!

Nevertheless, in the last few years, over 1,200 tote bags were made and transported to Australia or Spain for sale. A tag on each bag shows a picture of the woman who made the item and notes that 'fair-trade' wages were paid. An accompanying poster explains the reasons for the tote-bag project. However, we knew that relying on personal baggage allowances to transport the bags to Australia wasn't sustainable in the longer term. A better understanding of the local market system and higher productivity was needed if villagers were going to transform what was, until then, a subsistence farming economy.

In late 2019, we may have had a breakthrough. Amrita Craft agreed to stock and sell some bags through their fixed-priced shop in Thamel.

Ananta also offered to test the interest of his European customers in buying the bags. There had been an inquiry from an overseas buyer before the COVID-19 crisis closed borders in March 2020.

Despite the logistical difficulties and quality-control issues, the tote bag project has achieved its intended outcome of increasing women's family incomes. Between November 2017 and November 2019, twenty to twenty-five women in three villages have each made an average of AUD$90 to $100 over two bag-making sessions per year that coincided with our visit to Tawal, making approximately twenty-five bags per session. Each bag costs approximately AUD$5 to make, including materials and labour. COVID-19 forced us to reconsider how to transport the tote bags to Australia. In January 2021, approximately 500 tote bags and 100 aprons were air-freighted to Brisbane from Kathmandu at a cost of approximately AUD$2.40 per item. NAFA had been selling the bags in Australia for AUD$10, with the profit supporting NAFA programs in Nepal, including those in the Tawal area. The initiative provides an excellent seasonal income for the women so a decision will need to be made regarding whether to add the freight cost onto the selling price of the bags, risking a drop in the sales volume, or making less profit on the sale.

The strategy of appointing a Women's Social Mobiliser, however, has had mixed outcomes. Rebika held the position for two years, from November 2017 to November 2019. During our twice-yearly visits in that time, Rebika was extremely helpful in organising volunteers for the dental camps, collecting data on patients' oral-health status, helping organise the bag-making and payment, and organising women's workshops on topics such as family nutrition and financial literacy.

However, she had difficulty with the work in between our visits – the very issue Deb had intended her role to address. Rebika took no initiative herself, concentrating solely on monitoring existing projects and acting on Deb's suggestions. One or two women's meetings were held in between our visits but no reports of such meetings were received. Other ideas from women's group meetings during our visits, such as beekeeping, were never followed up. Women took part in training programs to grow cardamom and coffee, but these occurred through their membership of the Cooperative. They were not initiatives organised by Rebika. Overall, the intended outcomes of the position – generating ideas, strategies, markets, and new income-producing opportunities for women – did not materialise.

Finally, in November 2019, Deb met with Rebika to review her position. Deb had calculated that despite being paid the equivalent of a half-time position, Rebika had, on average, spent only twenty hours a month on women-related work. She spent her remaining time on her other paid job, collecting deposits for the Cooperative Savings Bank. The two-year position had run its course. Deb expressed her disappointment but told Rebika she hoped they could remain friends. Rebika, smiling nervously, showed little emotion but left looking very relieved.

On reflection, there are several possible reasons for this disappointing outcome. First, the Women's Social Mobiliser position was initially Deb's idea, and she consulted on it through Kanchha, the President of the HRDC. The proposal should have been discussed directly with the women's group to gauge and take account of their views. Second, the process of recruitment may have been flawed. Ironically, the HRDC's attempt to exercise due process produced the best candidate on paper but perhaps not the best candidate in the view of local women. The requirement set by the HRDC for Grade 12 qualifications precluded other women with some standing in the community from applying for the job. Rebika did not have a history of involvement with women in the area. She had just arrived back in Tawal, so was not well known locally. Perhaps some women felt resentment that the position went to a 'newcomer'.

Hints of possible resentment from some local women came out in the second year of the appointment. When pressed to produce updates on her work between our visits, Rebika expressed in a text message her own frustration that women were not cooperating with her:

> "First of all, women have to cooperate with me to do work. Like in goat project, they must rear and care for goat. They think they are on their own, but they must be cooperative [pooling ideas about goat-rearing]. By myself I cannot achieve goals. Women must cooperate. They [have to] get some interest to contribute to society."

Later, she said the women were resistant to having meetings:

> "The women are telling me 'why do we have to meet when we have work to do?' I am pushing women to make plans for beekeeping, and they said it takes time. If they cooperate with me, I can update you sooner."

Third, supervision proved to be inadequate. In face-to-face supervision, Rebika consistently denied any problems with her role and work. She believed she was doing a good job, explaining away many of Deb's concerns. Each time, Deb gave her the benefit of the doubt and set clear timelines for reporting. In the second year of the two-year initiative, Rebika communicated even less, adding to Deb's frustration. With the only communication the occasional Facebook Messenger comment, and Kanchha's limited time to assist, Rebika was struggling to fulfill her responsibilities. Perhaps with more face-to-face supervision and support, Rebika may have gained confidence and 'grown into' the position.

Finally, perhaps Rebika did not have the skills in report-writing and facilitating meetings that Deb had assumed from her application. Over time, it also became apparent that the women did not or could not follow through with written reports of meetings or details of their ideas for funding proposals. It is likely that the women needed training in leadership, meeting procedures, report-writing and the preparation of submissions. As numerous women's groups (mother's group, church groups, etc.) existed in the area, Deb had assumed they were active and productive, but this may not be the case.

Ironically, just as it appeared that no feedback on women's development would ever eventuate, the volunteer Women's Representative for the Ganga Jamuna Rural Municipality made a request to NAFA through Rebika for assistance in building a women's meeting room at Tawal. The broken-down monastery and private homes were not adequate venues for larger meetings. A financial contribution had been received from the Rural Municipality and additional funding was needed.

We discussed this request during our November 2019 visit. Deb's response was that the women had met just twice in a year, when we were visiting, with no minutes or proposals emerging from the group discussion. Deb indicated that without evidence of an active women's group to support such a proposal, NAFA could not co-fund construction of a meeting room at that time. The meeting room was eventually built with Ward funding.

Overall, the Women's Social Mobiliser position had some successes but the experiment was not as productive as hoped. We still felt there was a justification for such a position, with many unmet needs and issues in the community that warranted further investigation. Examples included early marriage, teenage pregnancy, and childcare for under school-age children. But modifications to the Women's

Social Mobiliser model were needed, and improvements could not be made without further discussion with local women. Those discussions would be delayed by the outbreak of the COVID-19 virus in early 2020 (see Postscript).

Overall, we tried to empower women by respectfully insisting on their participation, encouraging their ideas, and providing the funds for sound proposals. While we were mindful of the importance of feminist consciousness-raising regarding gender and societal oppression, we opted for an indirect approach. Women themselves felt men were largely supportive of their advancement, and thought poverty, rather than gender, held them back.

Chapter 17

Rebuilding economic livelihoods

Villagers were in shock after the earthquake. Lives and homes were lost. The earthquake also destroyed the infrastructure owned by the local Agricultural Cooperative, including two chicken sheds, a caretaker's cottage, and water and electricity connections. All had been built with founding Cooperative members' initial capitalisation funds, but there was no longer any spare capital within the Cooperative, or savings in the community, to pay for rebuilding.

When the earthquake struck, deposits stopped and villagers started drawing on their savings. They were not sure it was safe to rebuild in the area, and now, having also lost their investment in the Cooperative's infrastructure, their economic future was in doubt. The Cooperative had the potential, over time, to re-establish the economic livelihoods of local villages after the earthquake and create a pathway out of poverty for these subsistence farmers. Their experience, strength and natural advantage were in agriculture. They knew that they needed to diversify their crops, raise higher-value animals and improve productivity to bring in more cash income. But they were back to square one after the earthquake. Some extra support was needed to help the Cooperative rebuild lost infrastructure and regain momentum.

An application to rebuild the infrastructure owned by the Cooperative was submitted to NAFA in late 2016, and after receiving donations earmarked for that specific purpose, NAFA allocated AUD$15,000 towards the project. However, the restoration of physical assets alone would not enable the Cooperative to recover from the earthquake and reach its potential to transform the economic wellbeing of the local area.

A long-time NAFA supporter identified the English Family Foundation as a potential funding source for a grant needed to supplement NAFA's infrastructure grant. The Director, Allan English, was a well-known philanthropist with a passion for supporting economic development projects in remote and disadvantaged communities. In March 2016, Kanchha and Deb prepared a submission for funding to re-establish the Cooperative. The submission was successful, and in April 2016, funds were allocated to provide:

- A caretaker salary for twelve months
- Solar electricity for the chicken sheds
- The purchase of 700 egg-laying and broiler chickens
- Coffee-growing training and the purchase of a coffee-pulping machine
- Cardamom-growing training and the purchase of 20,000 cardamom plants for ninety farmers
- Goat-rearing training, the purchase of ten higher-value 'Jamunapari' goats and construction of goat shelters for a pilot group of ten particularly disadvantaged women
- Veterinary training.

The allocation was a big boost to Cooperative members, both practically and to the morale of a people still in shock from the earthquake twelve months earlier. They would be forever grateful to the vision of the English Family Foundation and the trust they showed in the Cooperative.

However, we were soon to discover something farmers around the world know – farming, like producing electricity and building earthquake-resistant classrooms, is a complex endeavour. It was time for us to gain an understanding and face the challenges of crop diversification, animal husbandry, productivity improvement and access to markets!

An example of how complex animal husbandry can be is the chicken business. From the beginning, chickens have been the Cooperative's main income-earner. It started with both broiler and egg-laying chickens. Raising broiler chickens was tricky enough. They had to arrive within three days of birth. Several baby chickens in each truckload would die in transit from the Terai, a lowland region in southern Nepal. The baby chicks needed to be vaccinated for the first five weeks of their lives. A small wood burner and solar lights kept the chicks warm at nights, when the temperature dropped and threatened their survival. The chickens have the run of a large shed but are not technically 'free range'. The local jackals would make short work of that scenario.

Broiler chickens require a specific diet at different stages of their forty-five-day lives. A company provides the chicks, the feeds and the medications (vaccinations and antibiotics). The farmers provide the housing and the labour. Antibiotics, including Doxycycline and Neomycin, are added to the feed to control chronic diseases such as E-coli, and every chick had to be vaccinated for Rani Khet (Newcastle) disease.

The Cooperative also had egg-laying chickens, but stopped this line of business on finding they could not compete with eggs produced on the Terai, where the farms are large and the owners control the price of baby chicks and feed. Even including the cost of transport, eggs off the trucks in Tawal were still cheaper than local eggs produced at the Cooperative.

We also discovered what farmers in Australia know very well – that crops need water to grow! Nepal's monsoon season lasts about four months (June to September), with the remainder of the year mostly dry. Access to water was needed year-round to sustain the newly planted coffee and cardamom plants, so watering crops had always been an issue that limited local agricultural productivity.

While in the area, the cardamom-growing trainer undertook a survey of the land owned by the ninety farmers who attended the training. He advised how many cardamom plants were suitable for the land each farmer owned. He estimated that a total of 10,000 metres of irrigation pipe was needed to irrigate the land to water the cardamom, coffee and other crops during the dry season. The Department of Agriculture had an incentive program that offered to contribute 50% towards the cost of the irrigation pipes.

NAFA asked farmers to also contribute a small amount towards the irrigation pipes. In December 2016, NAFA approved an allocation that, combined with the farmers' contribution, would cover approximately 50% of the cost of the pipes, expecting the remaining 50% to be matched by the government. NAFA also covered the cost of transporting the pipes to the end of the road head. After waiting several months in the dry season for the matching grant from the district office, the Cooperative decided to install what could be purchased with the funds provided by NAFA. Each Cooperative member received approximately half of their planned allotment.

Local farmers estimated that by the time the allocation from the district government arrived more than 12 months later, they had lost more than 20% of their cardamom and coffee crops due to lack of water in the dry season that followed planting. Nevertheless, Cooperative members were still confident of their decision to plant the crop, so much so that they had privately purchased another 25,000 plants in addition to the 20,000 funded through the English Family Foundation grant.

Feedback from Cooperative members on the cardamom and coffee-growing training was positive, and these crops have done well in the local soil and climatic conditions. However, it takes several years for coffee and cardamom plants to mature to the point where they produce coffee beans and cardamom seeds ready to market. Over that time, the prices of coffee and especially cardamom have fluctuated, with market prices based on global supply and demand. It is a risk inherent in farming around the world. Within a few years, though, the Cooperative had collected from members 300 kg of cardamom to sell in the market.

Before the higher-value Jamunapari goat program was established, a notice was published inviting expressions of interest from women wishing to participate in the program. The applications were then considered by the Cooperative Board, with ten women chosen to receive the initial distribution of Jamunapari goats, whose large ears and larger frame distinguish them from the local Khari goats. When the goats arrived, the Cooperative ran a lottery (one to ten) on who would be allocated which goats, as some goats looked stronger than others.

In accordance with the Cooperative's conditions for the pilot program, the first she-goat born to a Jamunapari goat is handed over to another poor family two to three months after birth. Every time a she-goat is born, members are informed and new applications are invited. Records were kept by the Cooperative for future follow-up.

Farmers pay 200 Nrs (AUD$2.50) to the Cooperative when a Jamunapari goat is sold. The Cooperative also owns a he-goat 'stud', which provides a stud service for local farmers' goats at a cost of 100 Nrs (AUD$1.25), whether or not the farmers are Cooperative members. The pilot program has provided a good income for both individual farmers and the Cooperative, and also seems self-sustaining, an important goal in community development. By January 2020, sixteen women were benefiting from the program, up six from the initial allocation. A total of twenty-five baby goats (kids) had been born, six she-goats and nineteen he-goats.

At a household level, we interviewed Prem Kumari, a woman who had netted 43,000 Nrs (AUD$538) through raising and selling Jamunapari goats.

> "I like to rear goats. After six months you get a new one. These new goats are bigger and sell well. With the money I earn I can manage my household well. I can buy food like rice, and things like school books and clothes. I have even been able to save 2,000 to 3,000 rupees in the Cooperative savings. I am making life better for my two children."

Kanchha estimated that the average annual income of a farming household was between 120,000 and 130,000 Nrs (AUD$1,500 to $1,625). For families with a Jamunapari, goats can bring in up to 35% of the household's total annual income.

A challenge for Jamunapari goat farmers is access to 'special' grasses such as Taki, Ipil and Nimaro, which the Jamunapari goats eat with other grasses and plants. Unfortunately, farmers had to walk up to a four-hour round trip, twice a week, to collect this 'special' grass. A limited amount had been planted on Cooperative land soon after the land was purchased. But a tree and plant nursery was needed to increase the supply of the particular grasses to Cooperative members.

The community also needed to plant trees that reduced the risk of landslide, increased the supply of wood for cooking, and helped to address the problem of deforestation in the area. The earthquake had exacerbated deforestation in Nepal. Even though as much timber as possible was salvaged and recycled, a phenomenal amount of timber had to be extracted from community forests and private land, or purchased from other areas of Nepal, to rebuild community infrastructure such as school classrooms and private homes.

NAFA successfully secured a second grant from the English Family Foundation to purchase and install a tree and plant nursery on land owned by the Cooperative. Higher-value crops, including coffee, would be propagated, along with grasses for animal fodder and fruit trees for earning income, supplementing diet and health improvement.

The original application was subsequently revised after an opportunity arose to purchase a high-tech nursery based on the 'fogger' system. The supplier, Sital Drip Irrigation Technology Industry, came up to the area for a site visit and quoted on a twelve-metre by six-metre nursery that would permit simultaneous propagation of more than 4,000 plants. Plants would be watered using a 'fogger' system, saving caretaker labour. The high-tech nursery was installed in December 2018. Within twelve months, plants being grown in the nursery or on Cooperative land included coffee, cardamom, cauliflower, 'developed' grasses, Sichuan pepper, turmeric, marigold flowers, apple, pomegranate, guava and chilli. This crop diversification will increase income-earning opportunities for Cooperative members and other farmers and provide nutritional benefits to local villagers.

However, the contribution the nursery would make to reforestation proved more challenging. In Chapter 8, we talked about discussions we had with district Department of Forestry officers in Dhading Bensi in 2012 about the plan to transfer the status of the main government-owned forest in the area to a community forest. It was proposed that the community forest above the village of Tawal be named the Pasang Chowk Community Forest. The transfer could only be effected through the development of a Community Forest Management Plan (CFMP) for the area. But progress sometimes takes a lot of time in Nepal.

Nine years later, in 2021, two government officers from the Forestry Department visited the Ward in which Tawal is located at the community's request. The community had identified and named three forests that they would like converted from 'national forest' (from which the community was banned from collecting wood) to 'community forest' in the following villages: Latab and Dhuseni; Tawal and Tawal Bensi; and Kutal.

The government officers were taken to visit each forest on foot and to talk to community leaders. They have returned to Dhading Bensi and the next stage is for the government to decide if they are willing to approve the conversion. That would trigger the next stage, involving the community working with the government to prepare a CFMP to detail how the community will both preserve and use the forest.

Once community forest status has been attained, the new nursery will be used to propagate fast-growing, shallow-rooted trees for firewood and building material, and deep-rooted trees to prevent soil erosion and landslides. The plants or trees will be sold at low cost to local farmers at planting-readiness stage to encourage uptake but also to ensure the sustainability of the Cooperative.

Chapter 18

Let's go to the market!

Access to electricity had provided new small business opportunities, with the establishment of a rural carpentry shop, a welder and a small bakery, all selling products to other villages in the area. The most progressive, risk-taking farmer in the area, Balsing Tamang, had begun to diversify crops, planting tea, coffee, cauliflowers, tomatoes, turmeric, potatoes and garlic. Balsing was also trying his hand at beekeeping. He had started to sell coffee beans to outside markets via agents. But again, it was small scale and, apart from coffee beans, largely targeted the local market. Thinking on a bigger scale was needed to grow the Cooperative and make it more sustainable.

In the lead-up to our November 2017 visit to the Tawal area, Allan English, a Brisbane-based philanthropist, asked if he and his friend Mike de Gruyter could join us for three days to look at the Cooperative. The English Family Foundation, in partnership with NAFA, had allocated funds to re-establish the Cooperative in the aftermath of the earthquake. We were honoured that he wanted to see firsthand how the Cooperative was operating. Kanchha emailed me in anticipation of their visit:

> "I hope you will provide some suggestions what we have to do on our side for Allan's visit to Tawal. I think Allan is more of a gentleman."

I replied:

> "Just be yourself and all others the same Kanchha. That is what Allan expects and will want."

Allan and Mike were impressed with the Cooperative model, and the leadership being provided on a volunteer basis by Kanchha, Balsing, Ramesh and others. They also recognised that Kanchha was a key change-maker in the community and that there was potential for further growth in the Cooperative. In responding to a question about further opportunities, Kanchha indicated that if he had more time to concentrate on these bigger-picture opportunities, the Cooperative would grow at a faster pace, reaching the point where sustainability into the future, without the need for outside financial assistance, was within reach.

The Cooperative had done very well during the early years of establishment and was recovering well from the earthquake. But it needed someone with vision and a solid track record in leadership to explore further market opportunities for Cooperative members. During our April 2018 visit, I asked Kanchha if he would be interested in taking a three-year leave of absence from his position as social studies teacher to take on a business development role in the Cooperative and lead a market system focussed Growth and Sustainability project. Kanchha's eyes lit up as he replied softly:

> "Rod, you know I love this place. I have many ideas but I am a teacher and have very little time. If I can do this agriculture work only, then we can make this a great place. Young people will want to stay here rather than go overseas."

The proposal, of course, would depend on whether project funding could be secured.

Cooperative members had some experience with bartering and selling produce in the local market economy. Local farmers also sold dokos to agents for markets outside the local area. However, I sensed that there was little understanding of how the market system worked outside the village. A project was needed that analysed the market system, identifying both market opportunities and market barriers, particularly for the poorest families in the area. Solutions could then be developed that helped villagers better access the market system. The analysis would incorporate questions such as:

- How does the market system work?
- What barriers currently prevent Cooperative members, particularly the poorest farmers, from accessing market opportunities?
- How can access to market opportunities or improved productivity increase cash income for families in the Cooperative?
- What could be done to ensure the Cooperative's sustainability into the future?

A market system framework would need to be developed to guide the project. On 25 May 2018, Deb and I attended an information session in Sydney conducted by the CEO of Palmera (www.palmera.org) on a market system development approach they called Village2Market. This information session and the model presented inspired me to adapt and simplify the model as a framework for the Cooperative that would become known as 'Bazaar Jaau' (translated as 'Let's go to the market'). My challenge was to simplify the complex market system into simple English, which could then be translated into Nepali and presented to Cooperative members in November 2018, our next scheduled visit to the area.

A four-page document was developed to guide the planned analysis of the local market system. Key concepts in that document included that *Bazaar Jaau* would have four main aims:

- Gain an understanding of how the market system works, including demand for local products.
- Communicate with various market players outside the boundaries of the local area.

- Make best use of local strengths to identify new market opportunities that increase cash income and strengthen resilience, particularly for the poorest families.
- Develop and implement strategies and solutions to increase productivity and reduce barriers that prevent local families from participating in the market economy.

As supply and demand in the market impacted on the income of Cooperative members, they needed to understand the market system in more detail and develop strategies that would create better market opportunities for them. The following graphic was developed in preparation for our November 2018 visit, to guide discussion with Cooperative members on what makes up the market system. Brief meanings of each component of the market system follow.

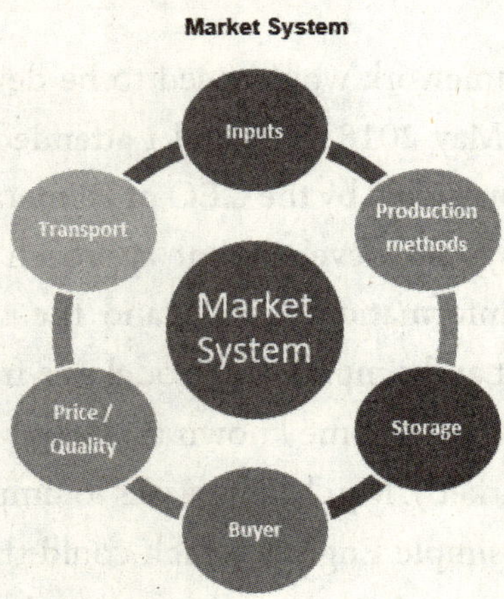

Market system

Components of the market system:

Inputs: Raw materials, such as saplings, water and fertiliser for plants or chicks, feed and medicine for animals.

Production methods: How crops are planted and harvested and whether any animals or equipment are used in the process.

Storage: How crops and products are stored before they are sold (for example, out in the weather or under cover).

Buyer: Who buys the products (for example, an agent or shopkeeper).

Price and quality: How price for a product is determined (for example, at a price set by an agent or by the government or a price negotiated between the buyer and Cooperative), and the impact that product quality has on that price.

Transport: How the products are transported to market and any limitations on that transport (for example, by truck during the dry season).

I also developed an overview of the Bazaar Jaau approach and a graphic. The graphic simplified the 'foundation' and 'pillar' elements of 'Village2Market'. The translated overview of the Bazaar Jaau approach included a brief description of its basic elements, as well as my observations of local strengths and challenges related to the Cooperative, starting with the 'foundation'.

Bazaar Jaau

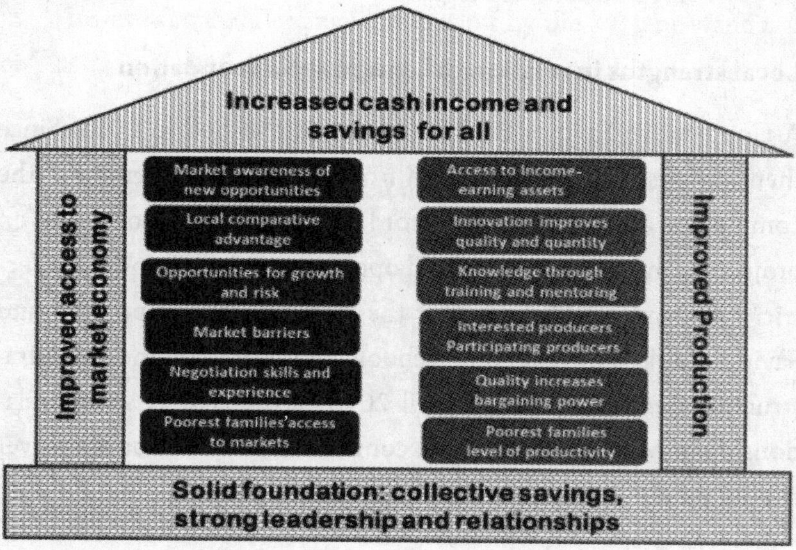

Laying a solid foundation

A solid foundation was needed before we could start a detailed analysis of the market system in which a village or group of villages operates. To lay this foundation, we would need to do the following within the community and between the donor INGO and the Cooperative.

Within the community:

- Establish a mechanism for building collective savings and encourage savings habits.
- Develop and maintain good relations among members of the community, who will collectively participate in and benefit from being in the Cooperative.

Between INGO and Cooperative members:

- Develop strong relationships with leaders and the community to ensure buy-in and support.
- Secure any funding needed to purchase assets or services for solutions/strategies.

Local strengths in relation to laying a solid foundation

A Cooperative Savings Bank had been established in 2013. Since then, savings had been collected from Cooperative members. The community also had a track record of working collaboratively on projects such as construction and operation of the micro-hydroelectricity system, establishment of the Agricultural Cooperative and Savings Bank, and rebuilding schools and other community infrastructure destroyed by the April 2015 earthquake. A strong relationship between NAFA and the community had been built up over twenty years.

Local challenges in relation to laying a solid foundation

Deposits in the Savings Bank had only recently started to recover. Even with these savings, the level of collective debt in the community was greater than total savings in the Savings Bank. Financial literacy training was needed. Family obligations represented a strength in relation to resilience, and also encouraged sharing that sometimes increased and at other times decreased the accumulation of savings.

Pillar 1: Improved access to market economy

The first 'pillar', or area of focus, is the market economy that operates primarily, though not solely, outside the boundaries of the local area. Important considerations in a systematic review of the market system include:

- Awareness of and access to markets and how they work.
- Local advantages/strengths which can increase income or reduce risk.
- Financial capacity to buy assets or services that could increase access to markets and/or improve productivity.

To progress, communities need both 'early adopters' and 'late adopters'. 'Early adopters' are local farmers who have the capacity to grow and take risks to grow even more (for example, by trialling new crops, developing and implementing innovations and expanding production). 'Late adopters' are local farmers who have the capacity and willingness to follow and take up ideas once there is evidence of success by the early adopters.

Local strengths in accessing the market economy

The establishment of the Cooperative was evidence of a determination to work collectively to diversify crops and increase cash incomes. Cooperative leaders, particularly Kanchha, also maintained a good relationship with the District Cooperative Office. The road had recently been extended to the area, which provided truck access to outside markets during the dry season (generally January to June and October to December).

Cooperative members have had some exposure and experience with coffee and cardamom buyers. An indication of the price they could expect for their coffee or cardamom produce was published by the government, based on the global price of the product. This reduced the risk of local farmers being exploited by buying agents.

Early adopters, including Balsing and Kanchha, are active leaders in the Cooperative. They have proven track records of being innovative and successful. They also have demonstrated a willingness to take risks and share knowledge with other Cooperative members.

Founding Cooperative members have experience with investing and depositing personal savings in the Cooperative Savings Bank, with more than 200 families following their lead. Nearly 100 Cooperative member households have also followed the lead of the early adopters and planted coffee and cardamom on their land.

The local soil in the Cooperative's catchment area, including that on land owned by the Cooperative, had been tested and was at the right altitude for some farmers to grow coffee and/or cardamom, two of the higher-value crops. Cooperative members like Balsing and Faising also had experience with introducing new crops to the area, such as coffee, tea and cardamom. High quality cane for making dokos was available in nearby forests.

Local challenges in accessing the market economy

While there has been some experience with outside buyers through the sale of baskets, goats and more rarely buffalos, there was limited experience with taking and selling products to outside markets. Women were dependent on support from Deb for purchasing material in Kathmandu and for selling tote bags in Australia. The recently opened road to the area was still closed during the monsoon season, with the duration of the closure unpredictable, depending on the timing and extent of monsoon rains.

Pillar 2: Improving production

Production can be increased through improved access to income-earning assets, such as land, irrigation pipes, fences, tools and equipment. It can also be improved through innovation that improves quality and quantity (yield) of crops/products. Such innovation can be gained through increased knowledge obtained from training programs and mentoring.

Improved quality strengthens the bargaining power of farmers, helping them obtain the best possible price for their product.

Extra support is needed for the poorest families in the community to improve productivity and access to income-earning assets. This helps overcome barriers, increasing the number of farmers interested in becoming producers who actually make the transition to active, participating producers.

Local strengths in improving productivity

Farmers have owned land in the Cooperative's catchment area for many generations. After the Cooperative was established, a district agricultural officer was invited to the area to test the local soil, altitude and other climatic conditions, and provide advice on new cash crops that could be grown in the area. With the help of a grant from the English Family Foundation, the Cooperative organised training programs for growing coffee and cardamom, as well as the raising of higher-value Jamunapari goats. Local, experienced and successful mentors, including Balsing, had a track record of supporting other Cooperative members by sharing knowledge of agricultural practices. Balsing had also long sold propagated plants to other Cooperative members at reasonable prices.

The Cooperative has introduced some productivity-improving assets that have increased the income-earning capacity of farming in the area. Irrigation pipes have been laid for farmers growing coffee, cardamom and other cash crops. A high-tech nursery has been installed to propagate new plants, crops and trees for income production and reforestation.

Finally, the community has a good track record in supporting the poorest families in the area. For example, school leaders encouraged the first-ever students from the low-caste Dalit (metalworker) families to complete Year 10. Community leaders also ensured that every poor family had access to electricity, even those unable to afford the connection fee.

Local challenges in improving productivity

Nevertheless, there were significant productivity challenges. Land in the area has been subdivided repeatedly into smaller and smaller blocks as sons were born, limiting economies of scale. Some families, particularly those from the Dalit community, have limited access to land and the finance needed to increase the capacity to produce. Farming techniques remain very labour-intensive. There may also be a shortage of labour in the future, as more young people are forced to leave the area to find work because farming is not profitable enough to support them locally.

While I was working on the market system and Bazaar Jaau training package, Kanchha and I exchanged emails regarding the development of submissions to the English Family Foundation and NAFA for resources to support the proposed three-year Pasang Chowk Agricultural Cooperative Growth and Sustainability project.

Kanchha identified the following aims for the project:

- Increase the number of families in the Cooperative.
- Increase the amount of savings in the Cooperative Savings Bank from 20 lakhs (AUD$25,000) at the beginning to 50 lakhs (AUD$62,500) by the end of the project.

- Coordinate the sale of all market goods outside the community to maximise the selling price for Cooperative members and provide a small commission for the Cooperative.
- Identify and arrange other areas of training that would increase market opportunities or improve productivity.
- Prepare a longer-term plan to ensure sustainability of the Cooperative for the next generation.

Kanchha and I jointly developed the first three-year budget forecast for the Cooperative, setting income and cost targets for coffee, cardamom, chicken meat, sale of plants/trees, and nett profit from deposits and loans to Cooperative members. The budget also incorporated the salary for a Savings and Loans Officer and a nursery caretaker/labourer, both funded largely by Cooperative profits, which were projected to increase over the three years and become sustainable beyond the project period.

The budget, consistent with the Bazaar Jaau approach that would guide the project, also included a provision for training and follow-up relating to new market opportunities identified, as well as a modest amount to purchase assets that would address barriers to accessing markets for the Cooperative, particularly the poorest families. The budget projections were ambitious for a fledging Cooperative recovering from a devastating earthquake, but as the project had only three years to achieve its stated aims, time was of the essence.

A submission was prepared for consideration by both the English Family Foundation and NAFA. In accordance with a request from Allan English and consistent with the sustainability theme, the contribution from the Foundation would decrease over the three years as the share coming from the Cooperative grew. The proposal was approved by the English Family Foundation in October 2018 and scheduled to commence in May 2019, giving the school time to recruit a replacement social studies teacher before the start of the new school year.

In November 2018, we took with us to Tawal two flexi-banners we had arranged to have made in Kathmandu. One had the market system graphic on it, the other the Bazaar Jaau graphic. The wording on the two banners was in both English and Nepali. Together with Kalpana, who was making her second visit to Tawal, and Pratika, we facilitated a workshop with Cooperative leaders to introduce the aims of the Growth and Sustainability project and the planned Bazaar Jaau approach.

The first item on the agenda was the proposal for Kanchha to work full-time as Business Manager of the Growth and Sustainability project. The collective response was a testament to the villagers' confidence in Kanchha.

> "Kanchha is doing so much work in the school, Cooperative and HRDC. If he moves from the school position that is a loss for our school, but it would benefit the whole community. We want this to happen."

As I explained the quite complex concepts of the marketplace system, I was conscious of doing a lot of talking. It was hard to know how the participants were receiving the information. I paused more often to ask the group what they thought about the ideas being presented. Their responses reassured us that they were understanding the concepts and how they related to the Cooperative.

> "We know in this country it is difficult to sell goods. We cannot solve everything. We will need a strong team working together to be independent. All committees

> must work together in partnership – if not it will be harder."

One participant identified the need for more promotion and explanation of the Cooperative system:

> "People need a good understanding of what is a cooperative. Do people really know what the aims of the Cooperative are? That idea has not spread. If they know more, they will feel like being involved."

The importance of pricing, quality control and profit were discussed.

> "Prices go up and down so we don't know until we are ready to sell what profit we might get. For example, the cardamom price is unstable. The price of dokos has fallen. Some took short cuts and our quality went down. Now people on the Terai are making good quality baskets and dealers are buying them at lower prices due to low transport costs. We need to find ways to increase productivity that save labour when making baskets but keep quality good."

> "The Cooperative needs to start making a profit so people get a return on their money invested. This will motivate others to join and to invest as shareholders also."

We also discussed with the teachers and with members of the HRDC the impact Kanchha's three-year secondment to the project would have on the school. Though expressing some concern over the pending loss, school leaders supported a project aimed at improving the economic wellbeing of the area.

When we returned home from Nepal, we met with Allan English. In the meeting, Allan suggested that a business plan be prepared for the project. The business plan would include next-step priority actions and performance indicators as well as three-year income and expenditure projections. It would also cover identified risks and strategies to mitigate those risks.

I developed a reporting package that would compare qualitative activity and financial data against the projections, working with the NAFA Treasurer to make the material as user-friendly as possible. I knew this important task would be very challenging for Kanchha, who would lead the project, Rebika Tamang, who worked part-time for the Savings Bank, and Ramesh, the Cooperative's bookkeeper.

Strategies were identified to minimise this risk. NAFA provided a new laptop computer to Ramesh Tamang to use for the project. I provided some bookkeeping headings to Kanchha and Ramesh that matched the three-year financial projections and would facilitate reporting. I planned to make two visits a year to the area during the three-year project and would provide ongoing advice to Kanchha and Ramesh regarding data-collection and reporting, though it was acknowledged that internet limitations in the village restricted the level of support that could be provided between visits. Only time would tell whether these mitigating strategies were sufficient.

Chapter 19

Buffalos, noodles, pigs and dynamos

Kanchha commenced full-time work on the Growth and Sustainability project on 1 May 2019. One of the main aims of the Bazaar Jaau market system framework (see Chapter 18) was foremost in his mind:

> "Make best use of local strengths to identify new market opportunities that increase cash income and strengthen resilience, particularly for the poorest families."

His first income-generating proposal was to establish a small buffalo milk industry. It would start with ten milk-producing buffalos and one 'he' buffalo. The milk-producing buffalos, suitable for the climatic conditions of the hilly region, are much larger than the local buffalos and would be brought in from other parts of the district. The buffalos would be owned and raised by women members of the Cooperative.

Milk produced during the nine-month pregnancy would be purchased by the Cooperative and sold to the local market (four villages initially), taking a small profit in the process. As the buffalo herd grew, the project would become self-sustaining, with some buffalos sold for meat and others kept for milking.

Milk-producing buffalo are expensive by local standards, so the proposal was for NAFA (through a grant from the Goldburg Family Foundation) to contribute 50% of the cost of the buffalo calves, including transport. The women receiving the buffalo calves would contribute the other 50%, funded by a loan from the Cooperative Savings Bank. Each farmer would also have to construct a buffalo shed on their private land.

Before the buffalos were purchased, the Cooperative requested a change to the plan. They proposed that five buffalos be allocated to women members of the Cooperative and that six buffalos (five cows and one bull) be kept on the land owned by the Cooperative, for milk and much-needed fertiliser. The Cooperative decided to convert the large broiler chicken house into a buffalo shed. After calling for expressions of interest, a young man was employed by the Cooperative to look after the buffalos and undertake other labour work in the Cooperative at a monthly salary of 11,000 Nrs (AUD$137.50).

As with the 'developed' goat program, the Cooperative called for expressions of interest for participation in the buffalo initiative. Fifteen applications were received, and the initial five successful candidates were chosen based on financial need, experience keeping a local buffalo, proximity of the buffalo shed to the road and access to the special grasses needed as feed. Expansion of the program would be managed the same way as the goat program, with the first female buffalo born passed on to another family.

The Cooperative Board selected women from three villages (Dhuseni, Tawal and Tawal Bensi) to receive the first allocation of buffalos. Women from the higher-up village of Latab were also interested, but wanted an allocation of four to five buffalos to make it worthwhile to collect milk early each morning and take it to the central milk-collection point in Tawal. The Cooperative agreed to allocate four to five buffalo calves to women from Latab when the opportunity arose.

A second income-generating idea, identified by women in the Cooperative, was the purchase of a noodle-making machine. The proposal was to make both wet and dry noodles locally. There was stable demand for the product – the women estimated that approximately 50% of families in the area ate noodles, currently bought in packets.

Under the proposal, the Cooperative would purchase the noodle-making machine. Housing for the machine would be built on land owned by the Cooperative. Training to operate the machine and package the noodles would be provided on site by the manufacturer. Noodles would be sold across twenty-five villages in the VDC (an estimated 1,400 families totalling more than 6,000 people) and to villagers in adjoining VDCs.

Villagers in the area would benefit by being able to access freshly made noodles at a lower price than they currently paid in the shop. Families would benefit, as the noodles would be made from wheat flour, without added preservatives or salt. The noodles would be healthier than packet noodles, especially when eaten with egg and seasonal vegetables.

Expressions of interest would be sought locally from women interested in working with other women to lease the machine from the Cooperative, manufacture both wet and dry noodles, and package, store, sell and arrange distribution of the noodles. The machine would then be leased to three or four women chosen by the Cooperative Board. Other women could be employed to sell and distribute the noodles.

A monthly rental fee would make the initiative sustainable, with the rental being used for maintenance and the eventual replacement of the machine. The rental fee would be determined once the machine was operating and there was an indication of the nett income earned.

In November 2020, a grant was received from the Tucker Family Foundation to purchase the machine. NAFA, in partnership with the Cooperative, provided funds to construct the housing.

Two other proposals were identified, aiming to benefit twenty families from the low-caste Dalit community. They speak Tamang but retain their own rituals and customs. Kanchha and I met with some of the Dalit men on one of our visits to the Dalit community. They indicated that they came to the Tawal area around 100 years ago. The Tamang people who were already there asked them to come because no-one else could make metal tools and other items. The older metalworkers explained the reasons for their migration to the Tawal area:

> "When Tamangs started staying here, they had food but there was no availability of metal things like pots to cook food, and Tamangs didn't know how to make them. So, they invited some metalworkers from Gorkha, Darke and Lapa to come here. Our ancestors had no proper place and no proper work. Where they used to live before was not a good place, and their economic condition was also extremely poor. That is why they migrated here for work and to make their business good. When we first came here, the Tamang community gave us land, helped us to build shelter and gave us food instead of money. They let us stay here."

Members of the Dalit caste have traditionally experienced significant discrimination when living in Hindu-dominated areas of Nepal, though this is not as pronounced within the Tamang community. Kanchha provided a few examples of such discrimination:

> "Dalit man can't come inside of other caste's house. Not enter in house. If any Dalit man came into another

> person's house to eat meal, he must sit outside alone. When he finishes his meal, he must wash his plate; then that plate is washed again by his host if from other caste. Members of other castes won't eat anything when visiting a member of the Dalit caste in his house. Finally, if a Dalit man touches water, that water is not drunk or touched by members of other castes."

Kanchha said that due to education and a long history of living together in the area, "90% of the 'bad attitudes' towards people from the Dalit community [have] disappeared in the Tawal area". Interviews of Dalit women in a 2011 social survey provided a mixed picture in relation to their community status but seemed to confirm this improvement in attitudes.

> "We are not discriminated from community, even though we are from lower caste."

The new national Constitution proclaimed in September 2015 banned discrimination against the Dalit caste, with one of the fundamental rights guaranteed being the Right against Untouchability and Discrimination (Article 24). Sadly, old habits die hard, but in the Tawal area, the families appeared well integrated into the community, at least to a greater extent than in other parts of Nepal. When we met with Dalit leaders to discuss initiatives that would improve productivity or open new markets for them, they told us that when they converted to Christianity several years ago, they no longer felt 'inferior' to other Nepalese.

Members of the Dalit caste living in the area traditionally married at a young age, with most of the girls then dropping out of school. Dalit girls often had their first child by the age of fifteen, which ended their studies and substituted the challenge of being a young mother. However, with the encouragement of the school, two male Dalit students had completed Grade 10 at Tawal.

One of the Dalit students was sponsored by another Nepal-based NGO to continue his study. NAFA and Smile Back to Me co-sponsored the second student, Deepak Biswakarma, after he attained the second-highest SLC result in the school. He completed an eighteen-month, government-accredited civil sub-overseer vocational-training course, which provided him with basic knowledge in the building-construction, water-supply, irrigation, roads, trails and bridges sectors. Deepak was then recruited into the Nepal Army as a sub-overseer. His family was immensely proud of his achievements.

A new proposal aimed at benefiting the Dalit community arose from a visit in November 2018 to the Dalit metal workshops. The suggestion was to purchase five electric dynamos (one per work group) to heat metal in the production of cooking pots and tools. Dalit metalworkers purchase iron and copper in sheets from Dhading Bensi. After the sheets had been cut to the desired size for the product, the iron or copper was then heated in one of two ways.

The traditional method was for metalworkers to push their left arm through the carcass of a goat skin, pumping to force air consistently through a small pipe onto the ashes under the metal being heated. The process required one person to undertake this task full-time. The repetitive manual action eventually caused pain in the elbow. We also saw them operate a small dynamo, which they purchased with funds provided by a local NGO. The metalworker manually 'pumped' the handle, again forcing the air needed to heat up the iron. While it did exert less pressure on the body, it still required one man to 'pump' the handle constantly all day. After little more than a year of constant use, the low-quality dynamo broke down.

The new electric dynamos were better quality, and could be used as the metal workshops had been connected to the local micro-hydro system. The metalworkers would pay a monthly tariff based on electricity usage but that would be more than made up for through increased productivity.

As Kanchha and I walked through the Dalit community prior to our meeting with Dalit metalworkers, I observed two Sunggur pigs lying in mud, being raised by a Dalit family. Kanchha indicated at the time that Tamang people traditionally did not eat much pork, but many, especially the younger generation, were starting to eat more. He said many in the Tamang community felt that the black pig meat of the Sunggur pig was more 'tasty' than the white meat from the Bunggur pig. However, many Tamang were put off by the hygiene standards displayed by Dalit families keeping the pigs.

A meeting with Dalit women was subsequently organised by the Social Mobiliser (Rebika). In that meeting, Dalit women told Rebika that it was the first time anyone had offered to meet with them as a group. The proposal arising from the meeting was to construct a concrete-floored pig pen and purchase one pig for each family. Interested Dalit families would be given the option of purchasing either the smaller black-meat Sunggur pig, which usually weighed 15 to 20 kg, or a white-meat Bunggur pig, which commonly weighed 30 to 50 kg. All eighteen families who subsequently chose to participate in the program preferred the Sungurr pig.

Under the proposal, well-drained, concrete-floored pig pens that could be kept clean with water would be constructed. Roofing sheets would provide shade for the pigs. A Memorandum of Understanding (MOU) would be signed by each Dalit family involved, stating that the project needed to be self-sustaining, with baby pigs being kept so that no further support would be needed from outside donors. The NAFA committee, while supporting the proposal in principle, had reservations, which we passed on to Kanchha.

In November 2019, we met again with members of the Dalit community to finalise the two proposals. In relation to the pig project, we wanted to make sure the proposal was supported by all villagers, not just members of the Dalit community. We expressed concern that the pig pens, with the associated noises and smells, would be constructed too close to the village centre, without adequate space for drainage. When we raised this matter at the meeting, one of the leaders in the Dalit community responded:

> "The pigs are too smelly to have in large numbers amongst our houses here. We will house them on small land holdings we have outside of town."

We asked for a written design of the pig pen, including the size of the concrete floor and the design of the drainage channels. We also asked whether the MOU the Cooperative was planning to sign with participating Dalit families would include any conditions to ensure the project was supported in the community and sustainable into the future.

After we returned to Brisbane, an MOU was developed by the HRDC and co-signed with each Dalit family taking part in the pig initiative. Conditions of the MOU included:

- Not all pigs would be sold, so pig farming would be continued on a sustainable basis.
- Nett profit from selling a pig and buying another piglet would be deposited in the Pasang Chowk Agricultural Cooperative Savings Bank.

- Savings from the pig initiative would be used for the health and education of the Dalit children, both sons and daughters.
- The savings in the Savings Bank would not be used to purchase alcohol, tobacco or other 'useless' items.
- Families would keep their homes and pig pens clean.

The conditions went further than we had anticipated, and it will be interesting to see the degree to which they are met when we evaluate the two Dalit initiatives in the future.

Chapter 20

We need a permanent marketplace

Improving access to outside markets in Kathmandu and elsewhere was one of the stated aims of the Growth and Sustainability project. With this objective in mind, Kanchha began making direct contacts with coffee and cardamom buyers and discussing with local farmers a proposal to pool harvested coffee beans and cardamom from Cooperative members in the hope of negotiating better prices for their crops. Three months into the project, Chandra identified both a current constraint to trading and an idea that would address that constraint.

> "Many farmers in the VDC only produce small quantities, not enough surplus to sell to outside markets. They need a permanent marketplace in the VDC at which farmers could sell their produce to other villagers."

Kanchha and I developed a proposal to establish a permanent marketplace in the Cooperative's catchment area, submitting it in September 2019 to the Australian Government's Department of Foreign Affairs and Trade (DFAT) for consideration in Round 2 of their Australian Aid Friendship Grants. Published information on the grant program indicated that applicants could expect a decision on funding in February 2020. The submission involved the purchase of a small block of land on the roadside and the construction of a marketplace shelter, a male and a female toilet, a water tap and a warehouse/storeroom.

A permanent marketplace, at which markets could be held on Saturday, Nepal's version of the Western weekend, would provide new sales opportunities for Cooperative members. It would stimulate trade between villages, offering an opportunity for local farmers and shops to barter or sell whatever surplus produce they had, such as various fruits, vegetables and local chicken. Kutal farmers could exchange bananas grown at a lower altitude with bamboo grown in Latab. Kutal farmers could sell rice and fish from the river. Farmers from Latab would sell potatoes. Larger quantities of surplus produce, including coffee and cardamom, would be sold to outside markets.

The Cooperative would be responsible for maintaining the land and managing the marketplace. It was envisaged that there would be approximately twenty-five stall-holders, who would pay rent to the Cooperative for the space they hired, helping the Cooperative maintain the site.

By the end of February 2020, there had been no announcement from DFAT regarding the Friendship grants. As COVID-19 struck Australia, government focus narrowed to responding to the virus. An email from DFAT received on 26 March stated:

> "We have made the decision to postpone the awarding of the Round 2 Friendship Grants due to the uncertainty and rapidly changing situation associated with COVID-19, including around travel arrangements… An announcement will be made as soon as possible about the program."

With access to funding from that source now in serious doubt, I decided to seek financial support from other sources, implementing the proposal in stages as money became available. Two of NAFA's loyal supporters offered to donate the funds needed to buy the land. It would take another ten months to source and purchase a suitably located site for the marketplace. The land (13 'Aana', or just over 400 square metres) was close to the road and just below the village of Tawal, so would be easily accessible. Chandra and Cooperative leaders would have preferred a larger block to accommodate future growth, such as more marketplace shelters. However, larger blocks were not available. Funds were provided by NAFA to purchase and flatten the land, with stone-filled gabion walls installed to strengthen the foundations for any buildings constructed on the land.

In June 2020, NAFA was successful in attracting a grant from the Goldburg Foundation to build marketplace shelters and install toilets and a water tap on the land. Simple plans were also drawn up and costed to construct on the land a building comprising a storeroom, office and small shop for the Cooperative. An application was submitted to the English Family Foundation proposing a funding partnership between them, NAFA and the Cooperative to construct the building. The submission was successful, and funding from the Goldburg Foundation, the English Family Foundation and NAFA was transferred to the Cooperative in late 2020.

Another significant milestone was achieved in early 2020. The Cooperative, under Kanchha's leadership, was successful in attracting the first state-level (called Federal in Nepal) grant received in the rural municipality. The Cooperative applied for a grant to expand and improve the productivity of their coffee venture in the area. Kanchha has reported that the application was rated the highest by the district office and was successful in a competition for funds amongst eight districts in Bagmati state.

The Cooperative signed an MOU with the government. An allocation of five lakhs 67,000 Nrs was approved to purchase:

- Four coffee-pulping machines for villages (Latab, Dhuseni, Tawal and Tawal Besi) in the catchment area.
- Twenty-five coffee-plant secateurs for members of the Cooperative.
- Two sheets of plastic sheeting for simple greenhouses that would increase the capacity of the Cooperative to propagate cardamom and coffee plants.
- 3,770 metres of 25 mm irrigation pipe for coffee and cardamom plants.
- Two sets of scales for the Cooperative to weigh coffee beans and cardamom.

The funds were now available to provide the infrastructure needed for a viable, sustainable permanent marketplace. It was up to the Cooperative to convert the vision into a reality.

Kanchha, President of the Cooperative and Business Development Manager of the three-year Growth and Sustainability project, reflects on the impact of progress in developing the Cooperative. When asked what difference the partnership involving the Cooperative, NAFA and Australian philanthropists has made to the lives of Cooperative members, he responded:

> "Local people's lives have changed significantly. In this earthquake-affected area, family incomes have increased from [the] sale of new crops such as cardamom and coffee, animal-raising including goat, pig and milk-producing buffalo-rearing. New small businesses have [been] started by members having access to loans through the Cooperative Savings Bank.

Farmers in the area know very well that to improve their incomes they need to learn together through a local Cooperative. They have received training in areas such as goat-rearing, pig-rearing and the growing of coffee, cardamom and other cash crops.

We have also learned about organic and non-organic growing of vegetables and fruit. Slowly, we are researching new ideas through our Cooperative. Having a local savings bank encourages local savings that provide safety in case of future challenges. It is also easier to obtain a loan to set up or grow a small business through the Cooperative.

The Cooperative Growth and Sustainability project has paid for local wages, both salaried and day wages, for both men and women. It also encouraged [us] and gave us confidence to apply successfully for the Cooperative's first grant from a Nepali government authority, one aimed at expanding and improving productivity in coffee-growing.

Our success is due to the partnership with NAFA and its supporters, particularly the English Family Foundation. The partnership provides needed financial support. We also learn from each other, sharing ideas with Rod, Allan, Mike and Bijaya. Rod has also provided management and market training for the Cooperative's board. We very much value that partnership. Thank you."

Chapter 21

Reflecting on community development success factors and challenges

We believe several success factors have contributed to transformative change in the Tawal area over the relatively short period of twenty years. These factors also helped villagers recover from the devastating Gorkha earthquake of 2015. However, significant challenges remain. The success factors and the challenges identified and discussed throughout this book are summarised here for those with an interest in community development practice.

Success factors

1. Understanding community and market system development frameworks

A community-based and then a market system development framework has guided our overseas aid practice in the Tawal area. These frameworks are comprehensive and multi-sectoral, covering areas such as water infrastructure, health, education, access to electricity, income-generation and agriculture. They also must be community-driven and organic, occurring at a pace set by the community and supported by donors within the funds available. The timeline needs to be flexible, decided by the community rather than the donor, though of course the project timing does need to line up with the allocation of funding. Development also needs to be sustainable over time, with an exit strategy developed so donor support is not indefinite.

To apply such an approach successfully, practitioners need to gain an understanding of the social, political and economic context in the host country of the community benefiting from the aid. They need good listening skills and cultural competence, which is the ability to communicate effectively and respectfully with people of other cultures. Practitioners also need negotiation and problem-solving skills, applied when working alongside community partners to identify and assess needs, priorities and solutions. Donors need resources available for timely allocations to address the highest-priority needs identified by the community.

Finally, practitioners need to have the resources and time to travel regularly to the targeted area to build relationships, meet with leaders, gain understanding of the issues, identify need, negotiate solutions and monitor implementation of one-off projects and ongoing programs. Continuity in that relationship is important to achieving good community development processes and outcomes. It takes time to build relationships and foster trust between donors and the community.

2. Being a member of an international-aid agency with good governance, a like-minded leadership team and a loyal network of donors and staff/volunteers

Every successful international-aid organisation needs good governance, including a leadership group that understands community and market system development and supports adopting that approach for at least part of their overseas project portfolio.

Every aid agency also needs a competent group of committed volunteers/paid staff and loyal, generous donors. Fundraising events are hard work and usually require an army of volunteers with the available skills and time to help. An awareness of potential funding sources and skills in submission-writing and reporting can bring in much-needed funds for specific projects. Prospective donors may be individuals from the general public, other like-minded not-for-profit organisations, private philanthropists, corporate donors or government international aid programs. Donors often have a passion and specific interest compatible with that of the aid organisation. They may also be willing and have the capacity to donate regularly for earmarked purposes, providing a reliable source of funds for multi-year programs.

3. Partnering and coordinating with other aid agencies

Small aid agencies like NAFA have a better chance to make a substantive, positive difference to people's lives if they are willing and have the skills to attract like-minded funding partners either from their own country or from other countries. In our view, aid agencies can achieve much more in partnerships than they can on their own. It has been our experience that many of the larger aid agencies prefer working on their own to partnering with others. At the very least, aid agencies should coordinate their separate aid efforts to avoid duplication. That requires good communication between the agencies and a willingness to share information – a success factor but in our experience also a challenge.

4. Identifying and partnering with cohesive, hard-working and transparent local communities

So much more can be done if community development practitioners are fortunate enough to work with open, honest, competent and hard-working community partners. Preferably, the partner is a local, volunteer-run NGO comprising members of the community who have a clear vision and share a passion, as well as understanding basic community development theory and practice. Transparency, mutual understanding and good communication are all essential ingredients to success.

The local NGO partner needs to be representative, with the support of the broader community. It also needs to have capacity and experience in community mobilisation. The local community must be active in any successful partnership with outsiders. Outsiders provide funds, encouragement and, at times, technical support, but the local community needs to have a vision and know what is needed. It also needs to have a track record of working cooperatively towards achieving that vision. A team spirit needs to prevail across the community, where community members want to mobilise and work together on both ongoing programs and one-off projects that will make practical improvements in the life of villagers in their community.

At an individual level, local change-makers who are visionary, competent and well-respected in the community need to be identified. They need to do their volunteer or paid work for the benefit of the whole community, not just for their personal interest. They are usually risk-takers and problem-solvers, with a clear and inspired vision of an overall plan or dream for the community. At the same time, they should be willing and have the ability to challenge their community, where required, and balance their expectations.

Community leaders are open to continuous learning as more information becomes available or mistakes are inevitably made. They believe in building community capacity and so are willing to share their knowledge and experience with others. Training, mentoring and the sharing of responsibilities strengthens capacity in the community, supporting sustainability.

Ideally, there should be multiple change-makers, so that neither the donor nor the community is dependent on one person. We have profiled strong, highly skilled change-makers in this book, but succession planning and the identification of multiple change-makers remains an ongoing challenge.

5. Trusting the abilities of community partners and being willing to take risks

We need to trust and respect the competencies of our community partners. Trust is gained through ongoing exposure, developing strong relationships and setting up reporting systems and processes that monitor the implementation of funded projects. We need to be flexible when changes to proposals are suggested by community leaders.

Community partners should also be encouraged to be open about problems encountered and mistakes made. In our experience, community partners are generally good problem-solvers, and everyone can learn from the occasional misstep. We can undertake feasibility studies, obtain advice from relevant experts, identify risks and develop strategies to mitigate those risks with our community partners. But in the end, regardless of the complexity of the project, we need to accept some degree of risk, trust the community and leave them to get on with implementing the project. The rewards are worth it!

6. Connecting with competent, supportive professionals and government officers

Successful community development practice requires networking skills to connect with the right person at the right time, to take advantage of opportunities, address barriers and solve problems as they inevitably arise. Community development practitioners need to connect, usually through their community partner, with government officers responsible for planning and monitoring in sectors such as education, health and agricultural development. Those officials can either assist community development efforts or set up barriers that present challenges and may impede successful outcomes. We have experienced both scenarios.

7. Measuring and evaluating outcomes

Allocating funds for ongoing programs and one-off projects is not enough. A monitoring and reporting system is needed to provide evidence of whether aid programs are achieving real improvements in the lives of aid recipients. Performance data (both quantitative and qualitative) needs to be collected either regularly or via periodic surveys or evaluations. Anecdotal evidence is rarely enough.

Evaluations should include analyses of available data and, where possible, interviews with those benefiting from the project or program. Donor agencies should be open to making changes that improve outcomes, based on feedback provided. Community partners should be encouraged to openly discuss problems encountered or mistakes made, so options for solutions can be discussed and lessons learnt from the experience. However, both the community and the donors need to be willing to drop or phase out those programs which are not sufficiently successful and where it has been agreed that changes are unlikely to turn the situation around.

Challenges

Not surprisingly, numerous ongoing challenges remain. We think they are likely to be challenges faced by many international aid agencies, both in their home country and in the host country of the aid program. Here are the challenges we have identified, but readers involved in aid programs can undoubtedly think of others.

1. Continuity in community development practice and expenses incurred

Adopting a community development approach requires regular visits and many hours of face-to-face meetings with community leaders, groups in the community who are particularly disadvantaged, and the general community where broader consultation is needed.

Practitioners need to be willing and have the time available to make the effort required.

For many, community development is their career and they are paid to undertake that work. For those practitioners, there are the traditional challenges of budget constraints, juggling work priorities and balancing work with family life. For those who are volunteers in aid agencies, there is an additional financial element to worry about, especially if out-of-pocket expenses are not reimbursed by the aid organisation. In NAFA's case, as with most small to medium-sized, volunteer-run INGOs, they are not.

2. Maintaining support within the aid agency for a community development aid approach

Inherently, community development has a long-term geographic and multi-sector focus. It often includes multi-year programs, such as support for education and/or health services. An overall vision and plan are needed, driven by the community but flexible and adaptable as unforeseen needs and opportunities arise. With that geographic focus, questions can arise within the aid agency as to whether too much time and funds are being allocated to a specific area, recognising that there is likely to be similar need in other parts of the host country.

Many aid agencies have a geographic focus, acknowledging that assessment and monitoring resources are limited. Support can be provided through one-off funding allocations for specific projects or annual funding allocations for multi-year programs. Other aid agencies have a sector-specific focus, such as education. That support often needs to be ongoing, such as through the sponsorship of local teacher salaries. Of course, many aid agencies have both a geographic and a sector focus (for example, supporting schools in a particular geographic area within the host country).

An Australian Ambassador to Nepal once advised, "Do what you do well and don't spread yourself too thinly". We are conscious of that wisdom, and NAFA has always supported a broad project portfolio benefiting several geographic areas that are accessible for assessment and monitoring. However, NAFA has also adopted a community development approach for one geographic area, the focus of this book.

At times, there has been some disquiet within NAFA regarding that focus, and others may experience the same. Over the years, we have done presentations to NAFA committee members and to NAFA's broader support network outlining a community development approach. However, corporate memory is often lost as supporters come and go. There is a need for refresher presentations. The ongoing challenge of maintaining support for community development related funding, including multi-year programs, will no doubt continue.

3. Supporting multi-year programs

The ongoing subsidy of salaries for secondary-level teachers and rural health workers remains a challenge. Several larger international aid agencies have a proven track record of raising enough funds, year after year, for their ongoing program commitments. It is more challenging for smaller, volunteer-run aid agencies like NAFA. We have been fortunate to have loyal and generous donors who have provided annual donations earmarked to our ongoing program commitments, but can that go on indefinitely? We are not sure, but the risk that donations may dry up must be considered.

The concept of self-sustainability works best for initiatives such as the micro-hydro project and the agricultural cooperative, which have a capacity to earn income. After help with set-up costs and support to develop and grow, both these projects should be self-sustaining. But teacher and health post salaries are more challenging. Student numbers for Grades 6 to 10 are fifty to sixty per class at the school in Tawal, justifying the allocation of additional government quotas for permanent teachers. But in Nepal, no doubt as in other developing countries, the education budget is insufficient to meet the national need and is not increasing. Budget limitations present a challenge to local communities and their supporting donors alike.

4. Communicating with villagers

There are only a few villagers in Tawal who speak English, and this is often the case in remote villages around the world. We manage with translators, but there is no doubt that we lose some of the nuances in translation and even at times something of substance. We are forced to put a lot of trust in translators to accurately present what we have said and report back the responses.

Communicating with community leaders in Tawal and other remote Nepali villages by internet or mobile phone also remains a challenge. Uploading or downloading documents, such as Excel financial spreadsheets or PDF project reports, is particularly difficult in these villages. This adds to the challenges of monitoring and evaluating the implementation of one-off projects and ongoing programs. As a result, much of this work must be done during our annual or twice-yearly visits to the area. COVID-19 has unexpectedly interrupted that routine, though the decreasing cost of international phone calls has helped maintain regular contact.

5. Succession planning for key change-makers in the community

Succession planning is another challenge commonly faced by international aid agencies. Often, significant time is put into developing and strengthening relationships with key change-makers in the community. Those individuals tend to be competent and well-respected by the broader community, so we add more to their workload, which they usually happily take on. However, unless those local leaders share responsibilities with others, and provide support through training and mentoring, capacity-building can be too narrowly centred on too few. A conscious effort must be made to broaden capacity-building activities and support. Succession planning is also essential, in case a key individual leaves the area, has a sudden illness or otherwise has his or her contribution to local development interrupted. But succession planning is easier said than done.

6. Managing the complexity of working across sectors

NAFA has supported the following initiatives in the Tawal area: water infrastructure, health, education, micro-hydro, improved cooking stoves, agricultural development, women's economic development and reforestation. To date, NAFA has had sufficient funds to address needs as they have arisen, but there is always a risk that in overseeing initiatives in numerous sectors, available donor resources are stretched or insufficient to respond to the needs identified by the community.

7. Improving rural health, including preventative health initiatives

Improving basic and ancillary health services in rural areas of Nepal, including oral, hearing and women's health services, is challenging. Health services are predominantly urban-focussed, as they are in developed countries. Encouraging health workers at the Tawal health post and dentists from Kantipur Dental Hospital to provide more preventative-health activities adds to the challenge. The health workers and dentists are technically very competent, and their training has undoubtedly focussed on those technical skills rather than on prevention. But new health-promotion strategies are needed to change entrenched health practices in the community.

There has been some success in NAFA's partnership with the Kantipur Dental Hospital. Urban-based dentists are being exposed to rural oral-health conditions, and a five-year tooth-brushing program in the early grades is increasing awareness and changing oral-health behaviour in young children. For older children and adults, however, achieving good preventative oral-health outcomes remains a challenge.

8. Addressing gender issues and mobilising women in the community

Working with women, one of the most disadvantaged groups in developing countries, is a key part of community development. This book identified some of the compelling reasons to invest time, energy and money in educating and empowering young girls and women. We have also identified initiatives that have benefited women and girls generally or specifically in areas such as education, women's literacy, women's health, animal-raising and tailoring.

However, engagement with women in the area continues to be a challenge. The employment of a Women's Social Mobiliser for two years was intended to increase women-targeted consultation between our annual visits, but the initiative had mixed outcomes and was not as productive as intended. We still feel there is a need for such a position, as there remain many unmet needs and issues in the community that warrant further investigation. Examples include early marriage, teenage pregnancy and childcare for under school-age children. But improvements to the Women's Social Mobiliser model are needed.

Postscript:

The novel coronavirus challenge

I flew over to Kathmandu on 22 January 2020 on a scheduled three-week visit. I was planning to accompany a dental group from Kantipur Dental Hospital who were going to conduct their fourth annual dental camp in the Tawal area from 3 February to 6 February. But it was not to be. On 16 January, something was picked up in a sleep study that concerned my doctor. She phoned Deborah just before I boarded a flight from Bangkok to Kathmandu.

Chandra met me at the airport and took me to Norvic International Hospital, where I saw a senior cardiologist. I had an ECG, blood tests and a twenty-four hour heartbeat-monitoring 'Holter' test. The cardiologist said some irregularities were found and she could not guarantee it was safe for me to travel to Tawal. She recommended a stress test and an angiogram. As there was no way Chandra would let me go to the village in those circumstances, I decided to pull the plug and return home. I was so disappointed, but I could see it was unfair to expect my hosts to be concerned about my health.

Unbeknown to me at the time, two days after I arrived in Kathmandu, a thirty-one-year-old student who had returned to Kathmandu from Wuhan, China, tested positive for the novel coronavirus disease. A day later, a positive test was recorded in Australia. On my journey home, I noticed that most passengers waiting to board flights at Bangkok airport were wearing face masks.

By the time I arrived in Brisbane on 31 January 2020, COVID-19 was becoming a big news item. After more tests and cardiologist appointments, I was medically cleared to continue with my plans, with the expectation that I would return to the cardiologist for an annual check-up. However, news of what was soon to be classified a worldwide pandemic was spreading fast. COVID-19 was about to cause devastating health and economic impacts worldwide, including in Nepal.

The WHO declared COVID-19 a pandemic on 11 March. The government in Nepal announced a countrywide lockdown on 24 March. On that day, Grade 10 students from Tawal school were in Satobato, five hours' walk away, in an adjoining rural municipality, sharing rented rooms and ready for four days of Secondary Education Examinations. They had been studying hard for these exams for the past five months, getting to school early for extra tuition. With the lockdown announced, students from all over Nepal were sent home, unable to sit their exams.

All international flights were stopped from 22 March, and Nepal closed its land border with China and India the following day. Nepal's first COVID-19 death was recorded on 14 May. In mid-May, the infection rate started to increase exponentially by more than 10% a day. By 6 June, there were 3,235 cases and thirteen deaths across Nepal and infections had spread to seventy-one of the country's seventy-six districts.

In the Tawal area, barriers to village entrances were set up, with only local villagers allowed in. Many returned to their village from Kathmandu, India and the Middle East when they lost their jobs. After a meeting of local leaders, it was decided that those returning home would need to quarantine in their homes, and in time a small quarantine room was constructed, attached to the health post in Salleri.

At a national level, coronavirus devastated the economy, affecting the tourist industry in particular. Locally, meetings of the Cooperative and the HRDC were suspended. Work on the rebuild of the health post also stopped, but was subsequently given approval by the Ward Representative to restart, as there were no active cases of the disease in the area and the health post was considered an essential service.

The road in and out of the area was closed, except for a truck allowed to travel to and from Dhading Besi to pick up a load of rice. The monsoon season then arrived, closing the road for another four months. The impact of the lockdown on the Cooperative's Growth and Sustainability project was mostly negative. Buffalo calves sourced for the milk-producing buffalo project could not be brought in from the Gumdi VDC, as coronavirus infection had been confirmed there. Similarly, the Cooperative was unable to bring in its usual truckload of baby chicks for raising broiler chickens, nor Sungurr pigs destined to benefit the local Dalit community. On the positive side, the Cooperative was able to sell an increasing quantity of vegetables to the local market because trucks were unable to bring in fresh produce from outside. Local farmers could till their fields but not meet in groups. With access to their own produce and isolated from outsiders, they were undoubtedly safer than those residing in the cities.

By October 2020, the infection rate in Nepal was doubling every month. Chandra's nephew Yuddha, one of our trekking guides and translators, had contracted COVID-19 and was self-isolating. Five or six houses in Chandra's neighbourhood had members with COVID-19, and one of these locals was in hospital on a ventilator. There were long lines in the few government-run hospitals that were providing free COVID-19 tests. In privately run hospitals, testing for COVID-19 cost more than 2,000 Nrs (AUD$25) per test. Under these circumstances, reported infection rates in the country were undoubtedly greatly understated.

After being given permission to open, the school in the village was soon closed again by the government. The city/rural divide in education grew wider, as private schools in the city areas, with better resources, offered their students remote learning, while government schools, particularly those in remote villages, were not able to do the same, due to poor internet connections and the few computers available to the schools and the students.

The worsening infection rate, however, improved in January 2021 when hospitals and vaccination centres began to administer, free of charge to Nepali nationals, the Covishield vaccine, a brand of the Oxford-AstraZeneca vaccine manufactured by the Serum Institute of India. One million doses of the vaccine were gifted to Nepal for the first phase, with another two million procured by the Nepal government. One million doses of that order were received. The priority for the first phase was front-line workers, with the second phase targeting people over fifty-five years of age. When the second million doses of the government's Covishield order failed to arrive due to the growing COVID-19 crisis in India, China provided 800,000 doses of their vaccine, Sinopharm. Targeted groups for the Chinese vaccine included front-line health workers, and staff employed in hotels, trekking agencies, the advertising sector and internet providers.

Infections began to increase rapidly in May 2021 due to spill-over from India. The national death toll from the virus reached 9,000, surpassing the number killed by the April 2015 earthquake. Lockdowns announced across the country extended into June, disrupting year-end school exams and forcing many out of work. The Nepal government reported that they urgently needed at least 1.6 million AstraZeneca COVID-19 vaccine doses to administer second shots. Authorities were forced to suspend the vaccination program after the country failed to secure fresh supplies of vaccine from India and China. In the next few months, China offered another million doses of vaccines after India banned exports of its AstraZeneca vaccine due to its rising infection rate. The government continued to scramble for vaccines, with the President of Nepal even writing to Russia's President Putin for help.

In June 2021, nearly eighteen months after the first novel coronavirus case was detected in Nepal, COVID-19 reached the former Ree VDC. Up to twenty COVID-19 cases were detected, including cases in Tawal and Kutal. COVID-19 patients soon took up the six beds in the government health post at Salleri, so the health workers there asked the health post at Tawal to start taking COVID-19 patients. NAFA funded the purchase of two five-litre oxygen concentrators and three oximeters, as well as replenishing personal protective supplies (N95 face masks, face shields, nebulisers and hand sanitiser), but early monsoon rains had already caused landslides, closing the road to the area. The order was put on road transport to the district capital, Dhading Besi, from where it was carried in dokos to Tawal. Once again, as villagers face new challenges, this time resulting from COVID-19, their indomitable determination and sense of community rise to meet them.

Thanks

First and foremost, I would like to thank Deborah, my wife and partner in everything, including the experiences documented in this book. From a trek to Nepal in 1999, we have come twenty years to sitting in our small study in Brisbane, Australia, back-to-back with our computers – both writing and fulfilling the various and varied responsibilities associated with a medium-sized, volunteer-run overseas-aid organisation. We ask each other for advice on issues and each expresses frustration with their computer. She has been an equal partner in all we have done in Nepal, and I am incredibly lucky to have had her support throughout, particularly in the aftermath of the terrible earthquakes in 2015. Deborah has also contributed to the writing of this book. She is the primary author of Chapter 16 'No house, no work, no livelihood', focussing on working with women.

Thanks also to Chandra Tamang, his wife, Pabitra, their three sons, Purna, Karma and Prabesh, and their live-in helper, Anu. Chandra has

been the main driver of change in the Tawal area for more than twenty years, and this story could not be told without his vision and determination. For several years, his wonderful family has hosted our stays in Kathmandu. We love Pabitra's cooking, and eagerly await news of what is happening with Chandra's family and neighbourhood.

Thanks also to the other main change-maker in this story, Kanchha Tamang. We first met Kanchha in Chandra's office, before Kanchha returned to Tawal to take up a teaching position after completing his studies. Kanchha became president of the local self-help group, and was the principal driver in establishing the local agricultural cooperative that has provided the area a potential pathway out of poverty. He learned English by watching BBC news on the television and is a visionary. Like Chandra, after experiencing the terrible earthquake that destroyed all infrastructure in the area, Kanchha then helped coordinate the rebuilding of four schools, a health post and agricultural infrastructure. Also like Chandra, this story would not have been written without his local vision, leadership and loyal support.

There are too many to thank in the Tawal area to name them all here – local builders like Buddha, Sirap, Kanchha Dong and Suk Lama, health workers Beg, Sunita and Lila Maya, Ward representative Faising, progressive farmer Balsing, and so many others.

In Kathmandu, a special thank you is due to Bijaya and Binu Rajbhandari, with whom we were connected by Mana Ranjit, one of NAFA's committee members. Both Bijaya and Binu have come to Tawal with us and been there to observe, learn and offer advice on the programs. They have both been very supportive of our approach in the area, and Bijaya has played a key role in fact-checking this book and providing his own input into the broader context within which this story has evolved. Others have come along just when we really needed them, so a special thank you to architect Sabin Shrestha, engineer Sadit Maharjan, geotechnical engineer Dr Megh Raj Dhital, Director of Kantipur Dental Hospital Dr Buddhi Man Shrestha, owner of Amrita Craft Ananta Gupta, and Joy Foundation Nepal directors Raju Shrestha and Babu Kaji Shrestha.

This story would not have been the same without the financial and other support provided by Raul Accion and his co-founders of Smile Back to Me, Alberto del Valle and Diana Jerez. Guenther Stummvoll and Christa Sprenger have provided similar, long-standing financial support from Austria. Vital assistance has also come from Kami Lama in France, Bikas in Belgium and our dear friends David and Ann Brown, then living in Hong Kong.

Back in Brisbane, the NAFA committee, including Nepal-born members, has been extremely supportive of the approach we have taken in the Tawal area. They provide advice, and raise funds for projects in Tawal and other areas of Nepal. Nepal-born engineers like Kamalayan Shrestha and others are also part of this story, providing technical advice and connecting NAFA with architects, engineers and other key expertise in Nepal. I am also incredibly grateful to those individual donors, too many to name, who have supported ongoing programs and one-off projects in the area that is the focus of this book. A particular thank you to Russ Waller for helping me with setting up the software programs (e.g. MailChimp) needed to market this book.

Heartfelt thanks are due to philanthropists, educational institutions and other INGO partners who have supported projects in the Tawal area, including the English Family Foundation, the Goldburg Foundation, the Queensland Independent Education Union, Partners in International Collaborative Community Aid, Queensford College, the Bangalow Country Women's Association and the Tucker Foundation. Allan English and Belinda Morrisey have contributed invaluable insights and support. They challenge, inspire and in the end demonstrate great trust in Balsing, Kanchha, Ramesh, and other Cooperative members working hard to grow the Cooperative for their benefit and the benefit of the next generation.

I am also greatly appreciative of the creativity of our nephew Morgan Denton Richardson, who provided the maps for this book, and Alison White, for her pedantic professionalism and patience in doing a very helpful and necessary copy edit of the manuscript.

A final and equally important thanks goes to friends and family, who have supported and tolerated what they have seen as both a passion and an obsession. We hope you can all come to see firsthand why we keep going back, year after year, and will do so while our good health prevails.

About the author and in-country adviser

Rod Setterlund OAM

Rod and his wife Deborah live in Brisbane, Australia, and have been involved with Nepal Australia Friendship Association (NAFA) since 2000. Rod has been President of NAFA since 2007, while Deb is NAFA's Research and Evaluation Officer. They have travelled to Nepal each year for the past twenty years (except 2021 due to COVID-19 travel restrictions), at their own expense, to work with Nepalese partners on NAFA-funded projects. Rod and Deborah were both awarded an Order of Australia Medal (OAM) in the 2013 Queen's Birthday Honours list in recognition of their service to the Nepalese people.

Rod with Bijaya

Rod was born in Canada. He completed a Bachelor of Business Administration, and qualified as a Chartered Accountant while working as an auditor for Price Waterhouse. He met Deb in Canada and in 1978 emigrated to Australia with her. After living and working as an accountant/administration trainer in Numbulwar, an Aboriginal community in northern Australia, Rod returned to the University of Queensland to complete a Master's degree in Social Welfare, Administration and Planning.

Rod worked for the peak community-based Queensland Council of Social Service before joining the Queensland public service. His career there spanned more than twenty years, working in policy, funding and management training relating to community-based services, including homelessness, childcare, neighbourhood centres, domestic violence and Indigenous-managed NGOs.

Since both Rod and Deb have retired from paid work, they have continued to volunteer with NAFA, a role that became even busier after the devastating earthquakes in 2015. Their other joy is sharing time with family and friends, and they are grateful that their two daughters (Kim and Angela), granddaughter (Heidi) and son-in-law (Scott) also live in Brisbane.

Bijaya Rajbhandari

Bijaya Rajbhandari is an engineer by profession, with post-graduate qualifications in environment management. He worked with UNICEF for more than thirty-five years, including eight years in Nepal. He also worked in eight different countries in Africa, Central Asia, South Asia and Far East Asia in the areas of education, health, nutrition, water supply and social policy. He was in a leadership position in UNICEF as Country Representative in Thailand and North Korea before retiring at the end of January 2016.

Bijaya's busy post-retirement life is mainly spent contributing in the field of social development, primarily as an advisor in the HelpNepal Network, a focal person for UNICEF retirees in Nepal, Vice-Chair of Former International Professionals of Multilateral Organizations, Chairman of Grande Social Foundation, which is a private sector-funded foundation, and contact person for NAFA in Nepal. He has travelled twice to NAFA-supported projects in the Tawal area to learn and provide advice. Binu Rajbhandari, Bijaya's wife, is also involved with NAFA, offering support to the students undertaking post-Grade 10 study in Kathmandu under the Further Education and Training program.

Bijaya and Binu both live in Kathmandu. They have two children. Their son, Bijene, is a physician and lives with his wife and daughter in Melbourne, Australia. Their daughter, Biva, is a public-health specialist with a social-work background and lives in Kathmandu.

Glossary of terms and acronyms

A note on the use of the words 'I' and 'we'

This book is primarily about the personal experiences of Rod and Deborah Setterlund. When the book refers to 'I', it is in reference to Rod. 'We' refers to Rod and Deborah.

Centre for Rural Technology, Nepal (CRT)

The Centre for Rural Technology, Nepal (CRT) is based in Kathmandu and has as its vision to develop, promote and disseminate environmentally sound renewable technologies.

Constitution of Nepal 2015

Proclaimed on 20 September 2015, the Constitution restructured Nepal into a federal republic, divided the nation into seven provinces, and completed the transition of Nepal from constitutional monarchy to republic and from a unitary system to federalism. The system of government is established with three tiers: federal, provincial and local.

Fundamental rights guaranteed in the Constitution and considered relevant to this book include:

- Right to Equality (Article 18)
- Right against Untouchability and Discrimination (Article 24)
- Right to Religious Freedom (Article 26)
- Right regarding Education (Article 31)
- Right regarding Health (Article 35)
- Women's Rights (Article 38)
- Children's Rights (Article 39)
- *Dalit's* Rights (Article 40).

Dhading district

Dhading is part of Province Number 3 (Bagmati) under the new Nepali Constitution, with Dhading Bensi as its district headquarters. The district lies north of the highway connecting Kathmandu and Pokhara. The most prominent mountain range on the northern boundary of the district is the Ganesh Himal, which borders Tibet (now China). Tawal falls within the Ganga Jamuna Municipality of the Dhading district.

Ganga Jamuna Rural Municipality and the former Ree VDC

Sometimes written as one word (Gangajamuna), this local body under the new Constitution was formed by the merging of four former Village Development Committees (VDCs), including Ree VDC, in which Tawal is located. According to the data collected on 2017 local elections in Nepal, the new Ganga Jamuna Rural Municipality has seven wards and a total population of 21,784 (Wikipedia).

Gompa

Buddhist monastery. The terms '*gompa*' and 'monastery' are used interchangeably in this book.

Hilly Region Development Club (HRDC)

This local volunteer-run organisation was set up in Tawal in the late 1980s to coordinate the planning and implementation of donor-funded projects in Tawal and nearby villages.

Hindu and Western calendar years

Vikrama Samvat, abbreviated as VS and BS, is the historical Hindu calendar used in Nepal and several states in India. To convert to the Gregorian (Western) calendar AD, subtract 56.7 years. Both dates appear in this book, though the Western calendar is mostly used.

Improved Cooking Stoves (ICS)

Improved cooking stoves (ICS) employ simple, inexpensive and widely used technologies designed to improve combustion efficiency of biomass (e.g. wood, cow/yak dung) and reduce exposure to indoor air pollution.

Khata

A greeting scarf that is given to family, friends or guests which show gratitude and wishes of happiness and prosperity.

Khola

River

Memorandum of Understanding (MOU)

A document signed between two parties (e.g. between a government department and an organisation or between an organisation and a family). The MOU sets out expectations on both sides and details the obligations and performance-monitoring standards the two parties to the agreement are expected to meet.

Mistris

Tradesmen such as carpenters, stonemasons, plumbers and electricians.

Nepalese Association of Queensland (NAQ)

A not-for-profit social organisation supporting people of Nepalese origin residing permanently or temporarily in Queensland, Australia. NAQ also has supported the Nepal Australia Friendship Association (NAFA) in its fundraising efforts over the years, especially following the devastating 2015 earthquakes in Nepal. See the NAQ website (www.naq.org.au) for more information.

Nepal Australia Friendship Association Queensland Inc. (NAFA)

An entirely volunteer-run overseas-aid agency based in Brisbane, Australia, NAFA was formed in 1989 after Expo 88. See the NAFA website (www.nafa.org.au) for more information.

Nepaleducaid

Guenther Stummvoll and Christa Sprenger established this informal, Austrian-based support group to raise funds for education-related projects in the Tawal area. Nepaleducaid has also been an important partner in the rebuilding of schools since the 2015 earthquake.

Nepalese money terms, foreign currencies and exchange-rate conversions

Nepalese money terms used in this book include:

- Nepalese rupees (Nrs)
- Lakhs (one lakh = 100,000 Nepalese rupees).

Exchange rates, of course, have varied over the years. For the sake of simplicity, the exchange rate in this book is assumed to be 80 Nepal rupees = $1 Australian (AUD$1) and one lakh = AUD$1,250.

Non-Government Organisation (NGO/INGO)

Also called community-based or not-for-profit organisations, (international) NGOs are often staffed by either or both paid staff and unpaid volunteers. They deliver a range of advocacy, humanitarian, development aid and other services, often in partnership with government bodies and/or other NGOs/INGOs in the donor country and/or the recipient (host) country.

Pasang Chowk Agricultural Cooperative and Savings Bank

The bank set up by and for members of the local agricultural cooperative in the Tawal area of Nepal. Deposits earn interest and fund loans to members of the Cooperative.

Ree Village Development Committee (VDC)

Also known as Ri or Rigaun (after the name of the village in which the VDC headquarters was located), this former local administrative body organised villages structurally at a local level. Each VDC was further divided into several wards, depending on the local population. For this book, Tawal and other nearby villages were in the Ree VDC, in the Dhading district. The VDC comprised nine wards and approximately twenty-five villages, of which Tawal, with some 200 families and a population of about 1,000, is the largest. VDCs were dissolved on 10 March 2017, following the proclamation of a new Nepali Constitution on 20 September 2015.

School Leaving Certificate (SLC) and Secondary Education Examination (SEE)

The Secondary Education Examination (SEE) is the final examination in Nepal's secondary school system, obtained after successful completion of Grade 10. It was previously known as the School Leaving Certificate (SLC). Every student must take this examination before continuing to higher secondary or intermediate-level education (Grades 11 and 12).

Smile Back to Me

Established by Raul Accion, Alberto del Valle and Diana Jerez to raise funds for education-related projects in the Tawal area, this informal, Spanish-based support group is another important partner in the rebuilding of schools after the 2015 earthquake.

United Nations (UN) World Food Program (WFP)

The UN World Food Program is the food-assistance branch of the United Nations. The world's largest humanitarian organisation, it provides assistance in emergencies, including conflicts and natural disasters.

World Health Organization (WHO)

The World Health Organization (WHO) operates under the auspices of the United Nations. Its primary role is to direct international health within the United Nations system and to lead partners in global health responses, including responses to natural disasters.